Fists & Flowers

Fists & Flowers

Leaflets from the Sixties

RICHARD HERTZBERG

Foreword by Robert Cohen

Edited and Designed by John Laursen

For permission requests, email the publisher,
with the heading "Attention: Permissions Coordinator," at the address below:
admin@thepublishingcircle.com
Regarding: Richard Hertzberg

FISTS & FLOWERS / RICHARD HERTZBERG
FIRST EDITION
ISBN 978-1-955018-99-9 (paperback)
978-1-955018-98-2 (hardcover)

In memory of my mother, Katherine Joseph

&

In appreciation of my wife, Christine Ambrose

Acknowledgments

FISTS & FLOWERS: LEAFLETS FROM THE SIXTIES evolved over a considerable period of time before reaching its final form and content. There were many individuals who supported the book's development in a variety of ways. I would like to express my sincere gratitude to the following people for sustaining me in this effort.

John Laursen, of Press-22 in Portland, Oregon, was closely involved with selecting the leaflets for inclusion and then restoring the digital files, provided valuable editing for all of the text, and designed the book.

Dale Leix and William Campbell applied their Photoshop magic to some of the most degraded leaflets and produced amazing results.

Robert Cohen, professor of history and social studies at New York University, generously provided an insightful foreword for the book based on his profound understanding of the various political, social, and cultural movements of the Sixties.

Janet Goldstein gave valuable advice on the book's elements, how to prepare a proposal for publishers, and strategies for approaching book marketing and publicity. At a critical juncture in the project, Karen Gatens offered helpful consultation and on numerous occasions stimulated me to reflect on my motivations for assembling *Fists & Flowers*.

In the early stages of contemplating a book presenting original source material from the 1960s I received feedback that sharpened and focused the book's substance from Charlie Bloomstein, Dave Dellinger, Greil Marcus, Jim Miller, Michael Rogin, and Michael Rossman.

I have been fortunate to have had decades of true friendship with David Brostoff, Korey Mandel, Bob Schnider, and Helene Schnider-Dobrer.

Jim Barron, Margie Arons-Barron, Jon Dobrer, Paula Friedman, John Judis, Steve Maizlish, Virginia Morell, Abe Peck, Stewart Slavin, Frederic Tubach, Sally Patterson-Tubach, and Mark Wexler, each an accomplished writer, generously took the time to review *Fists & Flowers* and provide endorsements.

Hazel, Sidney, Rick, and Triny Hertzberg offered, at various points in the book's evolution, encouraging and kind words that enabled me to push forward toward completion.

Photojournalist Howard Harawitz graciously allowed use of his iconic photograph on page 11 showing Jack Weinberg in the police car on October 1, 1964. Harawitz's large portfolio of images from the 1960s is worthy of extensive exploration.

Permission to use the photograph of Mario Savio on page 14 was obtained from the Associated Press.

The copyright owner for the photograph on page 16 of a student being arrested inside Sproul Hall is the Regents of the University of California, the Bancroft Library, University of California, Berkeley. This work is made available under a Creative Commons Attribution 4.0 License.

MANY OF THE LEAFLETS that appear in *Fists & Flowers* were from archives maintained by three institutions: the Bancroft Library, University of California, Berkeley; the Labadie Collection, University of Michigan, Ann Arbor; and Tamiment Library, New York University, New York City. The formal citation for each of these archives is as follows:

Social Protest Collection, the Bancroft Library, University of California, Berkeley.

University of Michigan Library, Special Collections Research Center, Joseph A. Labadie Collection.

Tamiment Library and Robert F. Wagner Labor Archives, New York University Special Collections.

Staff members at each institution were remarkably patient and informative in response to my many questions while I was conducting research for *Fists & Flowers*. In particular, I would like to recognize Julie Herrada (University of Michigan), Michael Maire Lange (University of California, Berkeley), Shannon O'Neill (New York University), and John Zarrillo (formerly of New York University) for their exceptional assistance in providing access to their institutions' leaflet archives.

FINALLY, I am so very grateful for Portland's radio station KMHD, whose hosts play an invigorating, eclectic selection of jazz music that has kept me sane and energized during many late evenings.

Contents

Foreword

MY LATE FRIEND TOM HAYDEN used to say that the last battle of the 1960s is the battle over memory. Hayden, jailed as a freedom rider in Albany, Georgia, where he began drafting Students for a Democratic Society's founding manifesto, the Port Huron Statement, went on to play a leading role in the movement against the war in Vietnam. Tom worried that the struggles of the 60s for participatory democracy and peace were being distorted and trivialized by persistent, slanderous attacks on the social movements of the Long 1960s and their legacy from the powerful American right wing. From Reagan to Trump, conservatives have been seeking to discredit those movements as purveyors of disorder and nihilism, and to undo the humane and democratic changes they helped bring to America.

In fact, it has long been a dream of the right to turn the clock back and make the egalitarian impact of the social movements of the Sixties disappear, which is what Trump's nostalgic campaign slogan "Make America Great Again" was all about. It is also what the right-wing-dominated Supreme Court has been up to as it has voided affirmative action, eviscerated abortion rights, assaulted the Voting Rights Act, and allowed businesses to discriminate against gays—decisions that aim squarely at erasing the gains achieved by the civil rights, feminist, and gay liberation movements. And, in one red state after another, laws and educational policies have been adopted that ban from their public schools discussion of controversial social issues, particularly on race and gender, deemed "divisive" by authoritarian conservatives. Such acts of political censorship are especially offensive to Sixties movement veterans, who in 1964 battled nonviolently for freedom of expression in the Free Speech Movement at the University of California, Berkeley.

Fortunately, as Hayden's words suggest, memory can serve as a powerful antidote to such acts of historical erasure, re-connecting us, in Abraham Lincoln's words, with "the better angels of our nature," and affirming the 1960s as an era when human rights in America were being expanded rather than repressed. Towards that end, Richard Hertzberg has put together an invaluable collection of revealing historical documents in *Fists & Flowers:*

Leaflets from the Sixties to remind us what the social movements of the 1960s were all about. The documents he has gathered are leaflets that were created and distributed by activists in the civil rights, black power, feminist, gay liberation, anti-war, environmental, free speech, and countercultural movements. Both the words and illustrations in these one–page handbills communicate succinctly what activists were thinking and what they and the various social movements sought to achieve. Here, then, are the genuine voices of Sixties activists as they battled for peace, racial and sexual equality, care of the earth, free speech, and more liberated and open lifestyles. The leaflets offer such passionate and eloquent expressions of political and cultural dissent that they speak for themselves. Readers also, however, benefit from the insightful introduction, commentaries, and historical contextualization provided by Hertzberg, which will help those new to this era understand the Sixties, the ideas and actions that yielded these rich historical sources, and the vision they embodied of a world free of war, bigotry, and social injustice. The combination of these engaging sources and Hertzberg's lucid exposition makes *Fists & Flowers* a superb introduction to the Sixties and its liberation struggles.

Although scorned by conservatives in both the media and the courts, diversity and inclusiveness are terms that embody one of the great strengths of *Fists & Flowers*, as well as the decade the book explores. Hertzberg understands that the history of dissent in the Sixties was far broader than the predominantly white, male-dominated New Left, and so his selection of leaflets emphasizes the rainbow of democratic movements of the Long 1960s, which featured women, African Americans, Chicanos, Asian Americans, indigenous people, gays and lesbians, and a range of causes from peace to the environment, to ethnic studies, to farm-worker organizing—and beyond politics to countercultural experiments with alternatives to the ethos and lifestyle of our competitive capitalist society. This richness is a reflection of Hertzberg's location in what was arguably the center of dissent in the Long 1960s, Berkeley, California, where from 1963 to 1971 he lived and picked up a vast trove of leaflets from political organizers and cultural rebels, which became the core of the historical materials for this book, supplemented by other leaflets he tracked down in key archives of social protest from coast to coast.

Hertzberg was drawn to leaflets as historical sources because, like the best authors of the new social history of the Sixties, he wanted to go beyond celebrities and convey how the protest movements looked to rank-and-file activists—and the leaflets, usually unsigned and anonymous, were generated by the movements themselves rather than by some famed leader. Indeed, the grassroots nature of these sources is affirmed by the fact that the leaflets literally belong to the public and were never copyrighted. All history is selective, and of the thousands of leaflets Hertzberg reviewed, he has chosen for inclusion in this book only those that best represent key dissident themes, issues, and events of the Sixties. Hertzberg embodies the democratic spirit of the era in working to make *Fists & Flowers* an accessible people's history rather than a dry and lifeless academic tome. The short, provocative leaflets, often incorporating dramatic illustrations, strike me as a quick and engaging way to help readers become acquainted with the extraordinarily wide range of protest activity and cultural criticism that characterized the Sixties.

The leaflets Hertzberg selected and published on these pages attest that the push for a more democratic politics and culture in the Sixties came not from elites but from ordinary people who organized themselves into mass movements to promote change. It was these movements that exerted pressure to end racism, sexism, and war making. When one considers that all of this was done with very low-tech tools—mimeograph machines, basic printing presses, phone banks, and leaflets—it is a testament to the power of grassroots organizing and democratic idealism to move masses of people. Indeed, my students—raised in the current age of text messaging, the internet, and social media—often express amazement and even disbelief when I explain that those enormous crowds of Sixties protesters photographed rallying against war and racism or on behalf of free speech were gathered not via personal computers (which had yet to be invented), but by the distribution of thousands of leaflets and face-to face communication involving dedicated activists working night and day on significant causes with intense personal commitment. The point here is not to idealize the activists of the Sixties, since they, like the rest of us, had flaws and made mistakes, but rather to suggest that the kind of energy and idealism that they displayed in winning democratic change needs to be matched if not surpassed in our own century if we are to save those changes from reactionaries who want to erase them.

At a time when one of America's major political parties has embraced an authoritarian cult of personality, these leaflets from the 1960s can serve as a valuable reminder of the power of democratic ideas to promote a more humane and egalitarian society. In this sense *Fists & Flowers* offers us not only a record of the past, but a hope for the future.

—*Robert Cohen*

New York City, Summer 2023

INTRODUCTION

Endings and Beginnings

Pacific Palisades, California

REFERRED TO BY RESIDENTS as "the Palisades," Pacific Palisades was, in the late 1950s and early 1960s, a sedate, isolated, White, mostly middle-class enclave at the far western end of Los Angeles. We moved to the Palisades from the New York City area when I was in the fifth grade. I attended the newly constructed Palisades High School, and spent summers at Will Rogers State Beach, known simply as State Beach, bodysurfing and trying to figure out how to approach girls. Over the decades and for many generations, State Beach has been a sacred adolescent gathering place.

My graduating class, in June, 1963, was the second one at Palisades High School. At eighteen years old, I was heading to the University of California in Berkeley to begin my freshman year. I had spent the summer after graduation in New York City. My roommates in the cramped apartment we shared in what at the time was known as the Hell's Kitchen section of Manhattan introduced me to the disorienting but revelatory effects of marijuana. Without knowing it, I was getting ready for Berkeley.

While in high school, our black-and-white television brought images of early civil rights demonstrations in the South to my sheltered, privileged world. Even though anti-discrimination protests were met with increasingly violent reactions from both the police and enraged White people, it all seemed quite far away. The Palisades was a remarkably placid, bucolic place.

The flight to Northern California from Los Angeles was a mere one hour, but in that brief time the environment of my teenage years faded quickly away below, literally and figuratively. There would be no more lazy summers at State Beach. My personal adolescence had ended and a historical epoch for the country was taking shape that would profoundly influence me and the lives of millions not only in the United States but around the world . . . the Sixties.

Leaflets Tell the Story of the Sixties

THE SIXTIES (1963 to 1973 for purposes of this book) was arguably the most contentious period in post-World War II American history. A primary ingredient of Sixties activism was the creation, printing, and distribution of leaflets. They were the most prolific, commonly used form of communication—the social media, as it were—of that time. Leaflets express and embody the unvarnished, spontaneous voices of the era. They are historical documents, encapsulating the passions and perspectives of the various political, social, and cultural movements of the Sixties.

Leaflets should be distinguished from posters. In general, leaflets are 8½ x 11 inches, printed in black and white, with informal design elements, and distributed by hand on street corners. In contrast, posters are larger, printed in color, intentionally designed for visual appeal, and commercially produced for display, advertising, or promotional purposes.

My initial encounter as a freshman with the campus of UC Berkeley was at the main entrance, the intersection of Bancroft Way and Telegraph Avenue. Walking through the intersection of Bancroft and Telegraph, on the right is Sproul Hall, the primary administration building, with Sproul Plaza and Sproul Steps forming a contiguous open space in front of this imposing structure. The palpable manifestation of political activism at UC Berkeley was most evident in these areas, and it was there that I and many other students were first exposed to leaflets as a form of free speech and expression.

Here, democracy flourished in a kind of open bazaar and forum with card tables, folding chairs, placards, and signs. Activists were handing out leaflets that had been produced on mimeograph machines or basic printing presses, and people were speaking, advocating, preaching, arguing, debating. A carnival atmosphere prevailed that was lively, vivid, and stimulating. This was in direct contrast to the buildings a short distance away, where thousands of students sat silently taking notes while their professors lectured. Thus, the first thing that students experienced upon entering campus, before getting to any classrooms, was other students giving them leaflets from organizations and groups advocating a multitude of positions.

During the Sixties, thousands and thousands of leaflets were handed out all across the country, most notably on and around college and university campuses such as the College of Charleston (South Carolina); Columbia University (New York City); New York University (New York City);, Rhode Island College (Providence); Temple University (Philadelphia); Tulane University (New Orleans); the University of California, Berkeley; the University of California, Los Angeles;, the University of Connecticut (Storrs); the University of Kansas (Lawrence); the University of Michigan (Ann Arbor); and the University of Wisconsin (Madison).

University of California, Berkeley, circa 1966. Photograph by Richard Hertzberg.

Leaflets were quick, easy, and cheap to produce. They cost nothing to disseminate. They were readily accessible and not subject to censorship or external control. They were, in short, the ideal means of publishing all types of anti-establishment messages and pronouncements.

Leaflets present the myriad causes and issues that animated the Sixties and constitute an extraordinary, profuse stream of statements and sentiments linked to the period's events. Leaflets record and reveal the raw immediacy and energy of the Sixties.

However, leaflets are not unique to the Sixties and in actuality have been a vital method of conveying attitudes and opinions since the Revolutionary War and continuing throughout American history. While they often present themes of dissent, the Sixties leaflets are really part of a long U.S. tradition of grassroots political and cultural communication.

The Library of Congress categorizes leaflets—also called broadsides, flyers, and handbills—as printed ephemera, which is "by far the most popular ephemeral format used throughout printed history." They are described by the LOC as

single sheets of paper, printed on one side only. Often quickly and crudely produced in large numbers and distributed free in town squares, taverns, and churches . . .

broadsides are intended to have an immediate popular impact and then to be thrown away. Historically, broadsides have been used to inform the public about current news events, publicize official proclamations and government decisions, announce and record public meetings and entertainment events, advocate political and social causes, advertise products and services, and celebrate popular literary and musical efforts. Rich in detail and variety, and sometimes with striking illustrations, broadsides offer vivid insights into the daily activities and attitudes of individuals and communities that created America's yesterdays. . . .

It should be noted that broadsides and printed ephemera express the language, experience, and viewpoints of the era in which they were published.

Characteristics of Leaflets

LEAFLETS ARE THE POLITICAL AND CULTURAL ARTIFACTS of the Sixties. They are unfiltered, unrestrained, and authentic, vividly reflecting the conflicts and concerns

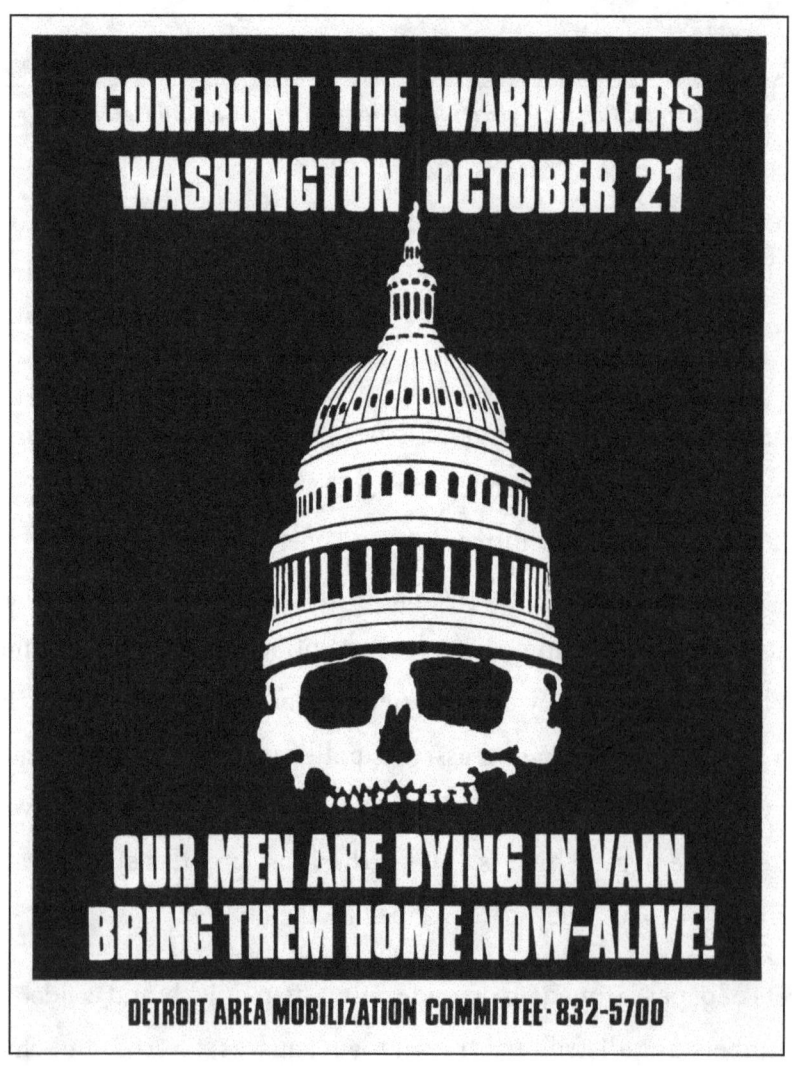

prevalent during the period. In both substance and appearance, each leaflet embodies an idea, a feeling, a mood, an attitude that somebody experienced. The leaflet is both the original expression and the lasting remnant of that experience. Leaflets were part of the historical process, a direct reflection of the flux and flow of the Sixties.

The leaflets varied tremendously, both in content and style. Some were carefully planned, coherent, and thoughtful statements from organizations. Others are the unmediated, defiant, strident outbursts of individuals who have seized, or were seized by, the emotions of the moment. They could be short and direct or ideological and bombastic. The leaflets embody the embryonic cries of rebellion that developed into radical assaults on powerful institutions and cherished beliefs.

Many leaflets have strong visual and graphic elements, ranging from the painfully unskilled to strikingly innovative and captivating. Some use multiple kinds and sizes of lettering scattered across the page, others are precise and orderly. A photograph, a drawing, a particular typeface or arrangement of letters, words, and symbols—all were used to complement and strengthen a leaflet's substantive content.

Perhaps the most compelling and prominent characteristic of the Sixties leaflets is their anonymity. The name or names of their authors or creators are rarely in evidence. Organizational affiliations sometimes yield clues regarding a leaflet's origin, although it should be noted that activist organizations during the Sixties varied considerably in size, structure, and longevity. Some were informal and brief associations of a few individuals. Others had specified leadership positions or roles, existed for several years, and claimed thousands of members (though frequently the definition of "member" was unclear).

What does stand out is that the anonymity of the leaflets amplifies their status as examples of genuine democratic populism. In the leaflets we literally see and hear "the people" talking rather than the recognizable leaders and spokespersons from the Sixties.

Structure and Organization of Fists and Flowers

IT IS DOUBTFUL THAT ANY ERA has produced such a diverse and eclectic repository of leaflets as the Sixties. Leaflets from the period were a raucous, exuberant, celebratory exercise of the First Amendment to the Constitution. They are tangible evidence that the Sixties were a vast experiment in free speech of every conceivable type.

With its profusion of activism, the Sixties probably witnessed the zenith of the leaflet, given the emergence and subsequent dominance of digital communications technology. Personal distribution of one-page paper messages has been replaced by the seemingly endless pathways of the Internet, e-mail, and the explosion of social media. It is highly unlikely that we will witness in the future the volume and variety of leaflets generated during the 1960s.

Fists and Flowers: Leaflets from the Sixties contains a hundred leaflets organized into seven sections according to the following categories:

Section 1: Civil Rights and Black Power

Section 2: Opposition to the War in Vietnam

Section 3: Ethnic Identity and Solidarity

Section 4: Women's Liberation

Section 5: Gay Rights and Sexual Freedom

Section 6: Ecology and the Environment

Section 7: The Counterculture

Each section starts with an explanatory overview discussing the issues, events, and themes referred to in that section's leaflets. There is a caption for every leaflet regarding its content, style, or historical context.

Background: UC Berkeley, 1963–1964

ON NOVEMBER 22, 1963, the country was stunned by the assassination of President John F. Kennedy in Dallas, Texas. This was quickly followed by the murder of Kennedy's alleged killer, Lee Harvey Oswald. Television presented both in real time. The violent deaths of Kennedy and Oswald definitively marked the Sixties for me and countless other young people. Like many my age, I was attracted to the youthful, articulate, intelligent president who had guided the nation through the 1962 Cuban Missile Crisis. His death abruptly ended our innocent teenage years and thrust us toward an uncertain future.

After Kennedy's death, UC Berkeley closed for the winter break and students went home to watch the memorable funeral ceremony for the fallen President—the bereaved Jackie Kennedy, the leaders from around the world who attended, the small Kennedy children waving American flags as their father's casket slowly passed by. Vice President Lyndon Johnson, a wily, experienced politician, became President, committed to carrying on "the Kennedy legacy." Part of that legacy, in Johnson's view, was to help South Vietnam fight Viet Cong insurgents and North Vietnamese Communists.

Returning to campus in early 1964, my friends and I wanted to resume our studies and some approximation of normal life following the shock of President Kennedy's murder. Spending those days at home sharpened the contrast between the peaceful Palisades where I grew up and the energetic, stimulating environment of UC Berkeley. Berkeley may have been about an hour by plane from the Palisades, but culturally they were on different planets. There was a striking difference between the quiet, isolated, White part of Los Angeles where innocent teenagers lived in stable family households compared to the vibrant, diverse student community in Berkeley where adult supervision was minimal.

In early 1964, political concerns became increasingly difficult to ignore or escape due to two emerging developments—spreading civil rights protests in the southern United States and growing turmoil in South Vietnam, where Buddhists and other dissidents challenged the U.S.-backed government and a broader civil war was intensifying. As the school year progressed, civil rights organizations were making plans for a "Freedom Summer" project in Mississippi, a formidable bastion of segregation and discrimination. A main focus of Freedom Summer was registering Black Americans to vote. In June 1964, hundreds of White college and university students made their way to the state and joined African American activists in this effort.

For three civil rights volunteers in Mississippi—James Chaney, who was Black, and Andrew Goodman and Michael Schwerner, who were White—the summer of 1964 was their

last. They were murdered in Neshoba County sometime between the late afternoon of June 21 and the early hours of June 22. The men who conspired to commit this atrocity were members of the Ku Klux Klan, the Neshoba County Sheriff's Department, and the Philadelphia (Mississippi) Police Department.

Nineteen sixty-four was also notable because it was a presidential election year. In a decision laden with irony, the Republican Party convention was held in the heartland of West Coast liberalism—San Francisco. Republicans selected a doctrinaire conservative, Barry Goldwater, as their presidential candidate. The Democrats chose the incumbent, Lyndon Johnson, and portrayed Goldwater as a reckless extremist who might start a nuclear war. Johnson, on the other hand, presented himself as prudent, practical, and personable.

In the years leading up to 1964, UC Berkeley students had expressed their political concerns by distributing leaflets, manifestos, and other written statements, affiliating with groups and recruiting members, speaking at meetings on and off campus, and organizing rallies and demonstrations. Starting in the mid-1950s, there had been numerous marches, picketings, and sit-ins throughout the San Francisco Bay Area opposing the proliferation of

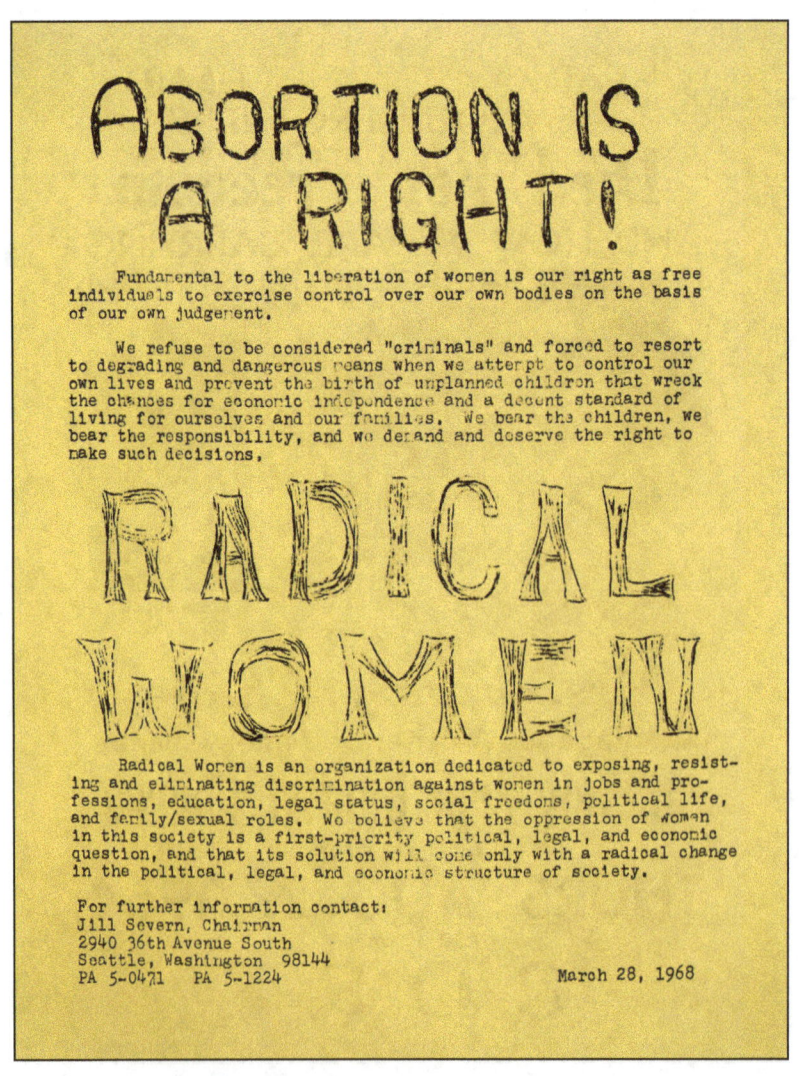

nuclear weapons, the House Un-American Activities Committee, the death penalty, discriminatory hiring practices by businesses, military recruitment on college campuses, and loyalty oaths required of professors. UC Berkeley students were prominent in these activities as organizers and participants. This history was perhaps on the mind of Clark Kerr, president of the University of California system, when he said on May 5, 1964, that "the University will not allow students or others connected with it to use it to further their non-University political or social or religious causes."

The Free Speech Movement

THESE THEN WERE THE CIRCUMSTANCES that preceded the return of students to UC Berkeley in the fall of 1964, when a conflict erupted over free speech—almost from the first day of classes—resulting in the formation of the Free Speech Movement. That dispute centered on the nature and extent of political activity students could engage in on campus, including specifically the distribution of leaflets publicizing and promoting actions occurring off campus.

The Free Speech Movement had a significant influence on the role that college and university students played in the political, social, and cultural upheaval of the Sixties. The FSM legitimized the free-speech rights of students at UC Berkeley, and by extension those at other colleges and universities. These institutions were the focal points for multiple forms of activism across the country during the Sixties. As they had been in earlier periods of American history, leaflets were an essential tool in the emergence and proliferation of that activism.

The seven sections of *Fists & Flowers* are deliberately broad, in order to portray the wide spectrum of initiatives that characterized the Sixties. The Free Speech Movement was, in comparison, narrowly concerned with the applicability of the Constitution's First and Fourteenth Amendments to student political activity on campus. Despite its subsequent national implications and impacts, the FSM as a topic did not fit logically into any of the book's seven sections. However, an examination of the FSM's evolution reveals that this major exercise of "student power" used strategies and tactics derived from civil rights struggles to establish college and university students as agents of change during the Sixties.

What follows is a description of the major elements of the FSM and an evaluation of the movement's importance. For further reference, an abundance of material is available at the websites of the Free Speech Movement and UC Berkeley's Bancroft Library. In addition, there is David Lance Goines' epic, meticulously detailed book *The Free Speech Movement: Coming of Age in the 1960s.*

The Initial Conflict

A NUMBER OF BERKELEY STUDENTS had returned to campus in the fall of 1964 after participating in the Mississippi Freedom Summer and witnessing the brutality of racism and the oppression of Black Americans firsthand. Others were energized by the accelerating civil rights crusade in the South and horrified at the slayings of James Chaney, Andrew Goodman, and Michael Schwerner during the Mississippi Freedom Summer campaign. Among activist students, there were discussions about organizing demonstrations in San Francisco, Oakland, and Berkeley, focusing on businesses with discriminatory hiring practices.

In what was likely an attempt to blunt this threatening possibility, UC Berkeley Dean Katherine Towle issued a letter on September 14, 1964, clarifying that the campus entrance area at the intersection of Bancroft Way and Telegraph Avenue was University property and emphasizing that it was thus subject to University rules and regulations. Henceforth those rules and regulations would permit only the handing out of informational materials; other forms of political advocacy or expression—setting up tables, soliciting funds and members, or giving speeches, for example—were no longer allowed. UC Berkeley administrators were especially concerned about organizing on the campus for off-campus political actions and activities, particularly those that could be considered illegal by civil authorities and might lead to arrests.

Subsequently, eighteen groups formed a United Front to oppose the newly enunciated policy. The United Front encompassed a wide spectrum of viewpoints, from Students for a Democratic Society and the Young Socialist Alliance to California Students for Goldwater and University Young Republicans.

The main thrust of the United Front was to emphasize the impact of the administration's position on freedom of speech and other Constitutional issues, and to minimize the ideological differences between the participating organizations. United Front members asserted that the First Amendment rights to freedom of speech and assembly, along with the due-process and equal-protection clauses of the Fourteenth Amendment, should be applicable on university property and for students on campus.

On September 30, 1964, students representing the Congress of Racial Equality (CORE) and the Student Nonviolent Coordinating Committee (SNCC) placed organizational tables at Sather Gate, just beyond the Sproul Hall administration building. This action resulted in the suspension of several students by Chancellor Edward Strong.

October 1–2, 1964

A NOON RALLY WAS PLANNED for October 1 in Sproul Plaza to protest the suspensions. It was in this area that Jack Weinberg set up a table for CORE, thus attracting attention from students coming to the rally. Weinberg had been involved with the Mississippi Freedom Summer project and had previously been a graduate student at UC Berkeley. Mario Savio, one of the suspended students, had also gone to Mississippi during the summer of 1964. Over time, he would emerge as a main representative of the FSM.

UC Berkeley police were dispatched in response to the situation. A police car carefully maneuvered through Sproul Plaza and the growing crowd of students who witnessed Weinberg being arrested and placed in the back seat of the vehicle. He practiced nonviolent disobedience, common to civil rights demonstrations, by going limp, neither resisting the police nor cooperating with them. Students quickly surrounded the car and sat down to prevent it from leaving. The sit-down was another technique borrowed from civil rights protests. More students entered the area of Sproul Plaza as Weinberg settled into the police car; he wasn't going anywhere soon. The university police report lamented that "the prisoner could not be removed from the car as the mood of the students had become ugly. He was left in the police vehicle."

Jack Weinberg, arrested and held in a University police car, October 1, 1964. Photograph by Howard Harawitz.

Students sit down on and around the University police car holding Jack Weinberg in Sproul Plaza, October 1–2, 1964. Photograph courtesy of Free Speech Movement Archives, Tom Kuykendall photographer.

In the hours over the remainder of October 1 and into October 2, the crowd swelled and the roof and hood of the police car became a literal stage for spontaneous remarks on the developing free-speech controversy. It was a remarkable scene that completely contradicted the paternalistic attitude held by administrators and many of the faculty: students should attend lectures, write notes, read books, study, and take exams—period. Instead, at this historic moment, young men and women, from middle- and upper-income families, dressed conventionally (it was 1964; dramatic changes in appearance, clothes, and hairstyles had not yet happened), violated the law and thwarted the arrest of Weinberg. For many of those involved this was utterly new territory. A line had been crossed and there was no going back.

At some point between October 1 and 2, the UC Berkeley administration decided that enough was enough. Hundreds of police from various law-enforcement agencies in the region mobilized near Sproul Hall. Seeing them gathering just a few yards away was, to be candid, both terrifying and exhilarating at the same time. The proximity of impending danger, combined with the intoxicating boldness of defying authority, created a high level of tension. What was going to happen next?

Seeing this scene evolve and sensing an imminent confrontation, some faculty members intervened to set up a meeting of United Front representatives with Chancellor Strong and Clark Kerr, the president of the entire University of California system. The result was an interim agreement for the students to end the demonstration around the police car and temporarily refrain from protesting. Weinberg would be charged with violating university rules and regulations, but not arrested or prosecuted. The administration would evaluate the status of the suspended students. And finally, all parties agreed to meet again soon to discuss the meaning of "free speech" on the Berkeley campus.

After thirty-two hours of confinement in the university police car, Weinberg was able to walk away peacefully. Equally significant, students had sat down across from two powerful University of California administrators and begun negotiations about their constitutional rights to engage in political expression and organizing on campus, as protected by the First and Fourteenth Amendments to the Constitution.

The Issues

IN THE DAYS FOLLOWING the police car incident, United Front members recognized that a more structured organizational identity was needed to legitimize their presence in upcoming interactions with the UC Berkeley administration and the wider audience of the university president and the Board of Regents, who made policy for all UC campuses. Thus, the Free Speech Movement was formed along with two leadership entities, an executive committee and a steering committee.

Specific issues regarding the status of free speech at UC Berkeley included the following:

- ◆ What was the scope of students' constitutional rights on campus?
- ◆ Did students need to get "permission" from the administration to exercise these rights?
- ◆ Did the UC Berkeley rules and regulations constitute "prior restraint" on student free speech?
- ◆ Could students advocate, recruit, and raise money on university property for off-campus causes and actions?
- ◆ Could students organize on campus for off-campus activities that authorities might deem illegal and where arrests might conceivably take place?

The basic position of the FSM leadership was that under the First and Fourteenth Amendments the university could not limit the content of speech by students on campus and could not prevent students from organizing on campus for off-campus actions.

The Stalemate

AS THE WEEKS WENT BY during the rest of October and then through November, 1964, the faculty was divided into factions with differing views and reactions regarding the FSM. There were traditionalists who saw the university as a sanctuary for rational, dispassionate debate and discussion in an apolitical, intellectual environment. They wanted to keep the campus and wider community separate, indeed thought that this was essential to the definition and role of a university in society. There were some faculty members who favored student free-speech rights and their exercise on campus but objected to what they believed were aggressive, confrontational methods of securing those rights—for example, the deliberate violation of rules or regulations concerning allowable political activity and expression, and protests of those rules and regulations through rallies, marches, and sit-downs. Still other faculty believed that the rights in the First and Fourteenth Amendments to the Constitution applied equally to students on and off campus and were explicitly supportive of the FSM's positions and tactics from the outset.

During this period, the UC Berkeley administration offered conflicting statements about whether students would be disciplined (by probation, suspension, or dismissal from the university) for past or ongoing political activity. In addition, Governor Pat Brown and the UC Board of Regents, the final authorities for the statewide University system, were becoming increasingly concerned about the ability of President Kerr and Chancellor Strong to resolve the free-speech conflict. Meanwhile, the FSM was attracting attention from the national media; popular entertainers and prominent civil rights figures were appearing in rallies at Sproul Plaza; and Mario Savio combined eloquence and passion to become the most visible voice of the FSM.

Mario Savio speaking at Sproul Plaza. Copyright Associated Press.

The FSM's position was clearly stated in a newsletter dated November 2 with an ominous warning:

> But let it be known that we can be stopped only by so many detours before the road begins to lead nowhere, and then there will remain one road, that of direct action.
>
> We demand these on-campus freedoms for all:
>
> 1. Freedom to advocate off-campus political and social action.
> 2. Freedom to recruit for off-campus political and social action.
> 3. Freedom to solicit funds for off-campus political causes.
>
> We expect to have full freedom of speech on this campus. There will be no settling for half of the First Amendment and two-thirds of the Fourteenth.

December 2–3, 1964: The Occupation of Sproul Hall

TO BREAK THE DEADLOCK in making progress toward defining the parameters and future of free speech and political activity on campus, the FSM's core leadership in the executive and steering committees determined that bold, dramatic action was needed. Such action would express a high level of commitment on the part of students to the principles and practice of free speech. At a rally on December 2, Mario Savio elevated the Berkeley free-speech controversy by framing it as a personal and generational struggle against institutionalized power with these electrifying words:

> There's a time when the operation of the machine becomes so odious, makes you so sick at heart that you can't take part! You can't even passively take part! And you've got to put your bodies upon the gears and upon the wheels, upon the levers, upon all the apparatus, and you've got to make it stop! And you've got to indicate to the people who run it, to the people who own it, that unless you're free, the machine will be prevented from working at all!

Singer Joan Baez was there. After she sang the civil rights anthem *We Shall Overcome*, students walked into Sproul Hall for an unprecedented sit-in protest and occupation. The floors and offices soon resembled the populist political arena at the intersection of Bancroft and Telegraph and in Sproul Plaza, with discussions, debates, and meetings spontaneously occurring in what was normally a center of bureaucratic functionality.

Representatives of the UC Berkeley administration admonished the students to leave the building, but that was not going to happen. Then, in the early hours of December 3, Democratic Governor Pat Brown, an acknowledged liberal, made the momentous decision to have

Student being arrested inside Sproul Hall, December 3, 1964. Photograph courtesy of Bancroft Library, University of California, Berkeley, Sid Tate photographer.

the Sproul Hall demonstrators arrested. The result was that starting on December 3 and continuing for hours, students were removed from the building. Some walked out willingly. Others were passively non-compliant and dragged or pulled down flights of stairs. They emerged into the daylight to be fully viewed by other students and the media. Accounts vary concerning the exact number of those arrested; it was somewhat more or less than eight hundred. Within a few days, they were referred to simply and respectfully as "The 800."

The Aftermath: Victory

As DESCRIBED PREVIOUSLY, the faculty was divided into factions, but the events of December 2–3 presented a stark contrast between the principled civil disobedience of youthful students and the presence on campus of hundreds of police from several law-enforcement entities who hauled those students out of Sproul Hall to jail. This caused many of the faculty to view the administration negatively and the FSM much more favorably than before. A leaflet, likely distributed on December 3, specifically called for the faculty to strongly support the FSM. The leaflet ended by invoking the civil rights refrain *We Shall Overcome.*

On December 8, the formal body of the faculty, the Academic Senate, held a critical meeting. They voted convincingly, 824 to 115, to endorse unrestrained political speech and advocacy on campus with no regulation or restriction on content and substance. In bold letters the front-page headline of a newspaper proclaimed "Powerful Academic Senate Backs FSM." On December 18, the UC Board of Regents, while not definitively endorsing the Academic Senate vote, did confirm that the protections of the First and Fourteenth Amendments to the Constitution applied unequivocally to student political activity on campus. The FSM had won.

Memory and Assessment

IN THE DECADES SINCE 1964, succeeding administrations of the University of California system and its Berkeley campus have, step by step, come to accept the FSM as a positive attribute of institutional history and tradition. Sproul Steps are now called Mario Savio Steps, as of 1997, with a permanent plaque to prove it. There is an FSM Café on campus, thanks to a generous contribution from Stephen Silberstein. The FSM Café features a photographic collage of FSM scenes and also praises the "passion, moral clarity, and democratic leadership style" of Mario Savio. The UC Berkeley College of Letters and Science has established the Mario Savio Memorial Lecture and Supporting Fund "to permanently honor the memory of Mario Savio and the moral courage, critical spirit, and vision that he and countless other activists of his generation exemplified."

All well and good, but my guess is that Savio would be a little uncomfortable with all the adulation and especially with the simplification of the FSM's rich, dynamic evolution into the actions and words of one person. Those "countless other activists"—where are the formal acknowledgments and remembrances of them? How about the eight hundred arrested in the Sproul Hall occupation? FSM stands for Free Speech Movement; there were thousands of students who supported and participated in it. How have they been officially recognized? The FSM cannot and should not become the story of just one person. This kind of reductionism minimizes the FSM's fluid, multi-dimensional nature, thus distorting rather than revealing and celebrating its character.

The fiftieth anniversary of the FSM, held from the end of September into early October, 2014, was an occasion to reminisce and reflect on its achievements and legacy. In that regard, Professor Emeritus Leon Wofsy, an early and ardent proponent of the FSM, made the following remarks at a September 27 panel discussion:

> FSM did win. Against stubborn and violent resistance from a paternalistic administration and a corporate-dominated Board of Regents, it won recognition that the First Amendment applies and is binding within the University. . . . And "free speech" turned out to be more than an abstraction. It sparked challenges to arbitrary authority; it soon merged into a powerful upheaval in opposition to the war in Vietnam. . . . In the aftermath of the upheavals of the '60s, the women's movement and the historic fight for gender and sexual equality burst through traditional restraints. The radical legacy of the '60s didn't begin or end with FSM. Nothing quite matches the remarkable heroism and overall significance of the civil rights struggle in the South, and of course FSM has recognized how much of its own inspiration flowed from that. . . . FSM turned out to be an important part of many lives, my own included. We have every reason to be proud of what happened at UC, of the spirit that added to the University's greatness.

Michael Rossman, who was a principal strategist, tactician, and then historian of the FSM and more generally the 1960s, referred to the leaflets of the FSM as "the paper lifeblood of our movement," in a section of the FSM website dated October 1997.

His comments about the FSM leaflets are also applicable broadly to the production, role, and impact of leaflets throughout the 1960s:

> You can also read the raw traces of our productive process — not only in the blotchy print of mimeos running low on ink and cheap stencils wearing thin as weary arms cranked the umpteen-thousandth copy through, but in the very words, in the typos and misspellings, the hasty and awkwardly precise phrasings, the mistakes typed over or just crossed out. Most of our leaflets were written at 3 a.m., after an afternoon meeting of the Steering Committee finally broke up, by a few of us who struggled to condense the meeting's sense to fit on a page, in time to rush this to the volunteer who stayed up to type the mimeo stencil in time to rush it to others who still stood by waiting to crank out the first thousand copies in time to give to those alerted by phone-tree last night to be ready at dawn to hand out the leaflets, smudgy with fresh ink, to students arriving for early classes at all the gates of the campus.
>
> By such means, as well as face-to-face, we spoke to ourselves about meanings, purposes, and urgent tactics, in a flood of paper discourse springing not only from the FSM's Steering Committee, but from all its other centers of organizing among the graduate students and teaching assistants, in the many departments and dorms, and from sympathetic ministers, Marxist analysts, crank visionaries, and dissident complainers. . . .
>
> We actually *believed* in the First Amendment, in the power of free speech. . . . Our leaflets were the exercise of our belief.

Perspective

Young, White, college and university students growing up in the late 1950s and early 1960s saw on television and in some cases personally witnessed the brutality and violence directed against African American civil rights advocates by other White people. We realized that the American promise of "equality and justice for all" was a myth, shown to be deeply hypocritical by the harsh realities of racism and discrimination. From the civil rights conflicts, we learned about tactics and strategies for nonviolent protest and about communication through the media and with those in positions of bureaucratic, institutional, and governmental power. The heritage of the civil rights movement not only permeated the Free Speech Movement at UC Berkeley, but in essence was the incubator for the opposition to the Vietnam War.

In turn, opposition to the war became the springboard for examining other issues addressed in the Sixties leaflets, issues that still reverberate across the nation:

- The role of military power in American foreign policy
- Imperialism
- Nationalism
- Power elites and oligarchy
- The use of force by law-enforcement authorities
- Poverty and economic disparities
- Discrimination
- Racism
- Sexism
- The unequal treatment of women
- Gay rights
- Ethnic pride and identity
- Community power, self-reliance, and integrity
- Environmental protection
- Resource conservation
- Materialism and consumerism
- Spirituality
- Healthy living
- The repression and expression of sexuality
- The dangers and benefits of mind-altering drugs

Two basic factors turned the Sixties anti-war movement into a spawning ground for a multitude of social, political, and cultural causes. First, the examination of U.S. intervention in Vietnam was preceded and stimulated by the challenge to our national mythology of equal opportunity and justice arising from the civil rights movement. Second, the anti-war movement generated a vigorous, relentless questioning of American actions in Vietnam. Further, a wide array of viewpoints converged under the vast umbrella of the anti-war movement, as exemplified by the leaflets in Section 2 of this book.

The ferment and unrest created by these two powerful dynamics fueled critiques of other domestic institutions and values, particularly among college and university students who were largely free of economic constraints and were living in environments that encouraged critical thinking and inquiry. What was set in motion was nothing less than a national self-analysis on many levels and in many arenas. This led to a comprehensive, penetrating evaluation of nearly every aspect of American society. The result is clearly stated in a manifesto from Students for a Democratic Society, shown on the following page.

The national self-analysis proceeded in different but parallel directions. "The Movement" was a broad phrase used to encompass and reference the myriad forms and facets of

SDS SAYS: FIGHT BACK

STUDENTS FOR A DEMOCRATIC SOCIETY, founded in 1962, is a multi-racial, international student organization dedicated to fighting against racism, imperialism, and the oppression of women. We ally with workers and students internationally, to help build these struggles. We are black, latin, asian, white, and native american. Membership is open to all who want to organize to fight oppression.

WE DEMAND an end to the political, military, economic, and cultural exploitation of Asia, Africa, Latin America, Middle East, and Europe, by the U. S. government. We fight to end ROTC, military recruiting, war research and all complicity with the war in high schools and on college campuses. We support the liberation struggles to throw the U. S. out of S. E. Asia.

WE DEMAND an end to racist exploitation of asian, black, latin, and native american and the acts of genocide perpetrated against them. We fight to end racist unemployment, racist textbooks, wage differentials, police brutality, welfare cuts, and immigration codes. We support ghetto rebellions and other struggles of minority people, and the fight for a minimum annual income of $6500.

WE DEMAND an end to sexism in its economic, ideological, and cultural forms. We fight for free legal abortions, free child care, equal pay for equal work, no sexist textbooks, no forced sterilization.

WE DEMAND decent working and living conditions for all. We will fight for 30 hours work for 40 hours pay, jobs for all, preferential hiring of all minorities and women, an end to the wage freeze. We support the right of workers to organize and strike.

WE SUPPORT the struggles of prisoners and other populations (such as retarded children, inmates in reform schools). We fight to end lobotomies and other nazi-like medical experiments. We support strikes and rebellions of prisoners to improve their conditions.

INDICT THE
US GOVERNMENT
FOR GENOCIDE

WE SUPPORT G.I.'s rights to organize in the Armed Forces against the brass. We support their right not to fight in imperialist wars. We support their right to refuse riot control training and to be used against domestic rebellions and strikes. We support G.I.'s struggles against racism in the Armed Forces. We demand full amnesty and repatriation for all who refuse service, are in exile, in stockades, or dishonorably discharged.

WE WANT TO IMPLEMENT these points by building a mass movement that fights on many levels. They would include militant mass actions such as strikes, sit-ins, picket lines, and confrontations; educational campaigns like forums, guerilla theatre, petitioning, canvassing, class room struggles, and debates; and legislation such as the anti-racism bill. However, we do not support individual acts of terrorism.

SDS CHAPTERS have a high degree of autonomy in deciding what struggles to be involved in. The above listed points are not exclusive.

WE WILL BUILD these struggles on campuses, in communities, in regions, nationally, and internationally!

Sixties activism, which was actually composed of many movements. Such terminology, though, does not begin to capture the complexity, the vitality, of that activism and those multiple movements. There are indeed distinct types of Sixties activism with their own features and agendas. Yet there was also a great deal of overlap between different parts of the Movement, with activities in one part influencing those in another. What gave the Movement much of its vibrant energy and variety was the ongoing formation, dissolution, and creation of groups, ideas, actions.

The Sixties' leaflets are a unique archive and repository illuminating the many strands of the Movement—a rich, evolving tapestry continually in motion—hence "the Movement." The voices that speak to us in the leaflets are raw, spontaneous, unrefined, passionate. Leaflets exemplify the remarkably diverse political and cultural activism of the Sixties. They express the intensity and impact of the conflicts from this period, conflicts that still persist in our present politics and culture.

SECTION 1

Civil Rights and Black Power

THE "CIVIL RIGHTS MOVEMENT," like the "anti-war movement," are terms indelibly connected to the period from 1963 to 1973—the Sixties. Both compress hundreds, even thousands, of events with enormous breadth, variety, and significance into simplistic phrases. Such phrases are useful, and are actually necessary for communicating, but they can also obscure the density and complexity of historical reality. Leaflets, in their authenticity, directness, and spontaneity, help to reveal some of the discrete actions and activities that exemplify and characterize the multi-faceted, overlapping movements of the Sixties.

Protests against the war in Vietnam fell largely within the 1963–1973 time frame. In contrast, civil rights activism was quite extensive prior to 1963 and continues today, decades later. Recall that Rosa Parks was arrested on December 1, 1955, for refusing to give up her seat to a White person on a public bus in Montgomery, Alabama. This incident sparked a boycott of the city's buses that lasted over a year.

Broadly speaking, the initial phase of African American civil rights protests focused on the historic inequities of discrimination, segregation, and voter registration, resulting in landmark federal legislation adopted during the Presidency of Lyndon Johnson (1964–1968) that was aimed at redressing those inequities. A related but distinct phase developed from the conception of "Black Power," which grappled with the legacy of racism on the cultural and psychological dimensions of African American life.

The civil rights movement during the Sixties is understood to encompass both of these different yet largely parallel phases. The leaflets in this section portray some of the different voices and elements that made up the civil rights movement from 1963 to 1973. In many cases, the realities of contemporary America remind us that progress is difficult to achieve, and once achieved can be thwarted or reversed.

For example, two leaflets promoting peaceful, integrated marches in Washington, D.C., during 1963 and 1964 refer to the filibuster as a barrier preventing adoption of a broad civil rights bill that President Johnson was supporting. The filibuster is unique to the Senate, allowing an individual senator or group of senators to talk interminably, trying either to delay or prevent voting on a piece of legislation. It takes sixty votes to end a filibuster, a threshold that is hard to reach. During the early 1960s, the filibuster was used by segregationist southern Democratic senators as a way to stall or sabotage civil rights legislation. The filibuster still exists today as a tool of obstruction.

A major legislative achievement of the Johnson Administration was the 1965 Voting Rights Act. Strikingly, this legislation was essentially voided by a 5–4 Supreme Court decision on June 25, 2013, *Shelby County* [Alabama] *v. Holder*. Two related sections of the Act, 4(b) and 5, were rendered ineffective by the *Shelby* decision, undermining the federal government's ability to exercise oversight on voting procedures and practices as implemented by states and local jurisdictions. What followed, and has actually expanded in the decade since, were a series of actions pursued by Republican state governments to redesign legislative districts and limit voting opportunities, tactics aimed at suppressing the vote among African Americans as well as among Hispanic and Latino Americans, Asian Americans, Native Americans, other "minorities," and college and university students.

The definition of "civil rights" and the "civil rights movement" evolved and expanded during the 1960s. The movement was, at first, a crusade with strong religious and moral overtones, which confronted the visible practices of discrimination and segregation in the South using an array of nonviolent strategies. In the August 28, 1963, March on Washington, Martin Luther King's memorable "I Have A Dream" speech and remarks by John Lewis, then a young activist with the Student Nonviolent Student Coordinating Committee (SNCC), nationalized what had been a largely regional protest and urged the federal government to adopt legislation that would end the most blatant forms of racial discrimination and segregation.

In a relatively short amount of time, the post-1963 civil rights agenda broadened considerably, in directions that moved well beyond a focus on discrimination and segregation in the southern United States. Black Power added a dimension to civil rights that focused on the internal development of Black communities rather than on integration. Black Power meant pursuing initiatives that prioritized self-determination, self-reliance, and self-empowerment for African Americans. Similarly, civil rights became associated with a comprehensive set of policies aimed at dramatically reducing economic inequality, redistributing political power, and celebrating cultural pride.

The meaning of Black Power, as articulated by such figures as Stokely Carmichael, Angela Davis, and Kathleen Cleaver, derived from earlier notions of Black and African nationalism linked to Marcus Garvey, W. E. B. DuBois, and Malcolm X, among others. Black Power was less concerned with traditional legislative demands but instead emphasized the psychological and cultural health of African Americans. Carmichael, for example, argued that it was necessary for African Americans to engage in protecting, building, strengthening, and bolstering their own communities *by themselves* in order to believe that they were equal to Whites. Without such experiences, Carmichael believed that integration would serve to reinforce the supremacy of White society and the dependence of Black people.

An early member of SNCC, Stokely Carmichael spent years participating in nonviolent demonstrations despite being beaten and jailed by police. By 1966, he viewed Black communities as ghetto colonies that had to be liberated, and saw a pattern of American oppression outside the United States as well:

> For a century, this nation has been like an octopus of exploitation, its tentacles stretching from Mississippi to Harlem, to South America, the Middle East, southern Africa, and Vietnam; the form of exploitation varies from area to area, but the essential result has been the same—a powerful few have been maintained and enriched at the expense of the poor and voiceless colored masses. . . . The need for psychological equality is the reason why SNCC today believes that blacks must organize in the black community. Only black people can convey the revolutionary idea that black people are able to do things themselves. . . . This is one reason Africa has such importance: The reality of black men ruling their own nations gives blacks elsewhere a sense of possibility, of power, which they do not have now. . . . One of the most disturbing things about almost all white supporters of the movement has been that they are afraid to go into their own communities—which is where the racism exists—and work to get rid of it. They want to run from Berkeley to tell us what to do in Mississippi; let them look instead at Berkeley.
>
> —*New York Review of Books*, September 22, 1966

An early expression of Black Power was the Lowndes County (Alabama) Freedom Organization, formed in 1965 as an alternative to the White power structure and Democratic Party in the county, the population of which was largely African American. The LCFO adopted the black panther as a symbol of strength and independence. It registered people to vote and ran candidates for county offices. In 1966, the more widely recognized Black Panther Party for Self-Defense formed in Oakland, California, and expanded nationwide. The Party also used the black panther symbol along with the display of guns as declarations of defiance and determination.

The Black Panther Party presented a curious mixture of revolutionary rhetoric imported from foreign sources, the brandishing of guns as a form of political and cultural assertiveness, and the operation of community centers that offered traditional social services.

Panther literature flirted with the advocacy of violence, using carefully calculated, ambiguous statements that were positioned between justifiable self-defense and armed insurrection. What united these seemingly disparate elements was the fact that they entailed Blacks acting together for themselves, without the direct involvement or support of Whites.

A leaflet issued shortly after the assassination of Rev. Martin Luther King Jr. on April 4, 1968, noted that he had "lived and died in the pursuit of social and economic justice for all. His last months were spent in the development of a Poor Peoples' Campaign to confront the nation with the desperate problems of poor people of all races." Indeed, King's viewpoint on civil rights activism enlarged markedly over the years prior to his murder. According to the leaflet, King was no longer simply challenging discrimination and segregation but now advocated for a larger civil rights agenda of "adequate income, responsible jobs, medical care, decent housing, a good education."

As a person with strong religious and spiritual beliefs, King struggled with moving even further—beyond proposing an enhanced definition of civil rights and an alliance of the dispossessed, to taking a position against the Vietnam War. Criticizing America's Vietnam intervention might weaken support within the United States for overcoming the racial prejudice, economic disparities, and cultural biases that hindered African American advancement. Further, such criticism would also put King into direct conflict with President Lyndon Johnson, his ally in pressing for sweeping civil rights legislation.

Ultimately, King could not resist his own awareness and growing conviction that self-determination for African Americans at home should also mean self-determination for Vietnamese abroad. Oppression and repression, as perpetuated by American practices and policies, must be resisted, regardless of geography. On April 4, 1967, exactly one year before he was shot dead in Memphis, King publicly articulated his opposition to the Vietnam War using moral and ethical language, arguing as well that the war was draining resources out of the country and away from domestic priorities. King avoided simplistic radical rhetoric and slogans—"Cops Out of Vietnam, Cops Out of the Ghetto," as one leaflet proclaimed—but he had in effect merged the civil rights and anti-war movements into a unified force that demanded, in the words of another leaflet:

- ♦ Immediate and total withdrawal from Vietnam;
- ♦ Self-determination for Vietnam and Black America;
- ♦ Ending all forms of militarism;
- ♦ Ending racism and poverty;
- ♦ Ending the draft; and
- ♦ Prioritizing social needs, not war.

King's speech in April, 1967, opposing America's military involvement in Vietnam, transformed the civil rights agenda from securing constitutionally guaranteed rights to challenging economic and political injustices, and went on to articulate a broad critique of American imperialism, militarism, racism, elitism, and materialism that was, in the end, similar to the perspective of Stokely Carmichael.

The evolution of the civil rights movement has continued over the succeeding decades. It is a long way from legislation that addresses rights already stated in the Constitution, such as the right to vote, to exposing and confronting systemic and institutionalized bias and prejudice, poverty and deprivation, economic inequality, educational underachievement, repeated incidents of police abuse and violence, and intentional disenfranchisement through legislative redistricting or gerrymandering.

The explosive convergence of the civil rights movement with the anti-war movement led to a widespread examination of American society and the rapid development of separate but related movements for change. The civil rights demonstrations of the late 1950s and early 1960s taught White activists much about protest strategies and tactics, lessons that were largely applied to demonstrations against the Vietnam War and went on to be used in other arenas by Hispanic and Latino Americans, Asian Americans, and Native Americans, women, the LGBTQ community, environmentalists, and countercultural rebels.

Julian "Cannonball" Adderley   John O. Killers
James Baldwin   Viveca Lindfors
Harry Belafonte   Gerry Mulligan
Theodore Bikel   The Chad Mitchell Trio
Dave Brubeck   Robert Nemiroff
Diahann Carroll   Mike Nichols
Ossie Davis   Maynard Solomon
Ruby Dee   Pete Seeger
Art D'Lugoff   Nina Simone
Dr. Burt D'Lugoff   George Tabori
Jules Feiffer   Dan Wakefield
Lorraine Hansberry   Shelley Winters
Nat Hentoff

PRESENT:

TONY BENNETT   HERBIE MANN SEXTET
OSSIE DAVIS   CHARLIE MINGUS
RUBY DEE   THELONIOUS MONK

and
The Students' own
FREEDOM SINGERS

IN:

"A Salute To Southern Students"

For their courageous, dedicated and
persistent struggle for Human Dignity

****

F R I D A Y ,   F E B R U A R Y   1ST,   1 9 6 3

8:00 - 11:30 P. M.

CARNEGIE HALL, 7th Avenue and 57th Street, N. Y. C.

Tickets Priced from $2

Presented as A Benefit for

THE STUDENT NONVIOLENT COORDINATING COMMITTEE

On the third anniversary of the Sit-Ins, the Student Nonviolent
Coordinating Committee and its New York friends will present
a program at Carnegie Hall. The benefit will support students
working in such hard core rural areas as Georgia where churches
have been burned and Mississippi where students have been shot
while working in voter registration.

SNCC, Room 1025, 5 Beekman Street, New York City CO 7-5541

The Student Nonviolent Coordinating Committee was one of the main civil rights groups that organized African American voter-registration campaigns and demonstrations to protest racial discrimination and segregation at businesses and facilities in the southern United States during the late 1950s and early 1960s. This benefit features a multi-racial group of prominent actors, musicians, singers, and writers from the period who came together to acknowledge and support SNCC.

JAMES FARMER
Congress of Racial Equality

MARTIN LUTHER KING
Southern Christian
Leadership Conference

JOHN LEWIS
Student Non-violent
Coordinating Committee

A. PHILLIP RANDOLPH
Negro American Labor Council

ROY WILKINS
National Association for the
Advancement of Colored People

WHITNEY YOUNG
National
Urban League

MARCH ON WASHINGTON

WEDNESDAY AUGUST 28, 1963

America Faces a crisis...

Millions of Negroes are denied freedom...

Millions of citizens, black and white, are unemployed...

Discrimination and economic deprivation plague the nation and rob all people, Negro and white, of dignity and self-respect. As long as black workers are disenfranchised, ill-housed, denied education and economically depressed, the fight of white workers for a decent life will fail.

Thus we call on all Americans to join us in Washington:

- to demand the passage of effective civil rights legislation which will guarantee to all
  - ...decent housing
  - ...access to all public accommodations
  - ...adequate and integrated education
  - ...the right to vote
- to prevent compromise or filibuster against such legislation
- to demand a federal massive works and training program that puts all unemployed workers, black and white, back to work
- to demand an FEP Act which bars discrimination by federal, state and municipal governments, by employers, by contractors, employment agencies and trade unions
- to demand a national minimum wage, which includes all workers, of not less than $2.00 an hour.

JOIN THE MARCH ON WASHINGTON FOR JOBS AND FREEDOM
and become part of the great American revolution for human freedom and
justice Now.

(Local Affiliate)
The Lower Eastside Civil Rights Committee
119 Suffolk Street, New York 2, New York

For bus tickets and transportation subsidies;
Phone GR 3-2193

MARCH ON WASHINGTON FOR JOBS AND FREEDOM

Approximately 250,000 people participated in the March on Washington for Jobs and Freedom, where they heard Rev. Martin Luther King Jr. deliver his legendary "I Have a Dream" oration. A young John Lewis, a founding member of the Student Nonviolent Coordinating Committee, also spoke to a notably integrated and peaceful crowd. The march was intended to emphasize the need for national civil rights legislation to address such issues as voter suppression, discrimination in employment, and school segregation. The leaflet states that Black workers and White workers both suffer when "discrimination and economic deprivation plague the nation."

CITIZENS OF SOUTHWEST GEORGIA

THE CONSTITUTION OF THE UNITED STATES SAYS:

1. Anyone born in the United States is a citizen of this country and the state where he lives.

2. All citizens of the United States have a right to vote that no state can deny because of race or color.

YOU ARE A CITIZEN
YOU HAVE A RIGHT TO VOTE

FOR A FUTURE IN SOUTHWEST GEORGIA

REGISTER AND VOTE
AT YOUR COUNTY COURTHOUSE

SNCC: Student Nonviolent Coordinating Committee

The Student Nonviolent Coordinating Committee was in the forefront of voter-registration campaigns throughout the American South during the early 1960s. The leaflet's focus and language are modest, restrained, and limited in scope, simply encouraging people to exercise their constitutional right to vote.

HEAR!   HEAR!
HOW OUR BROTHERS
Died For Freedom
AND HOW WE ARE CARRYING ON THE FIGHT IN MISSISSIPPI

Mickey Schwerner   James Chaney   Andrew Goodman

HEAR
Mrs. Fanny Chaney
Courageous Mother of James Chaney
At New Zion Baptist Church
2319 THIRD STREET
THURS., AUG. 27, 1964
7:30 P. M.
C O R E

In 1964 national civil rights groups, local churches, and community organizations organized the "Freedom Summer" campaign in Mississippi, a main focus of which was voter registration. Young White men and women came to the state to work with Black activists. June 21–22 proved fateful for civil rights organizers Michael Schwerner, James Chaney, and Andrew Goodman. They were pulled over, arrested, severely beaten for several hours, and then shot to death in Neshoba County by a group of men affiliated with the Ku Klux Klan, the Neshoba County Sheriff's Department, and the Philadelphia (Mississippi) Police Department. (CORE was the Congress of Racial Equality.)

BACK TO WASHINGTON, D. C. FOR CIVIL RIGHTS LEGISLATION JUNE 15, 1964

A united leadership of the churches, civil rights groups and labor in the New York Metropolitan Area has set June 15 as the day when it calls upon us to return to Washington to raise our voices for passage of the Civil Rights Bill — **now.**

"This March", said the leaders in their Call issued May 20, "will be the symbolic voice of many men of good will raised in moral indignation against the sin of segregation, prejudice, and injustice — a crusade calling for the end of the disgraceful filibuster now desecrating the Senate Chamber".

Last August, when tens of thousands of us went to Washington to demand passage of the Civil Rights Act, we pledged to return as often as necessary to secure our goal. The time has come to redeem that pledge **now.**

In Washington we plan a day of peaceful, non-violent **action** for civil rights. We shall march to the Capitol, visit Senators, monitor the Senate debates, and engage in a silent vigil. We shall hold a public meeting to review and explain the vital meaning of this Civil Rights bill for **all** of us, North and South.

"Though this bill is far from perfect, we urge its passage nevertheless, for it will provide at least this minimum of legal protection whereby men can continue their struggle in the streets and in the courts".

DON'T DELAY. Contact your church or synagogue, your Civil Rights organization, your women's club, youth or fraternal organization, and your labor union. Make arrangements to come to Washington June 15 by bus or train. Make sure that your voice is heard in the nation's Capitol!

JOIN THE
NEW YORK MARCH TO WASHINGTON FOR CIVIL RIGHTS LEGISLATION

CITY WIDE HEADQUARTERS:
13 ASTOR PLACE, NEW YORK 3, N.Y. OR 3-5120

CO-CHAIRMEN
Rev. Edward T. Dugan*
 Resurrection Roman Catholic Church
Rabbi Alfred L. Friedman*
 Union Temple of Brooklyn
Rev. Eugene Houston*
 Rendall Memorial Presbyterian Church
 * Co-Chairmen of the Com. on Race & Rel. of the Com. of Rel. Leaders of the City of N. Y.

SPONSORING CHAIRMAN
Rev. Edler G. Hawkins
 St. Augustine Presbyterian Church

TREASURER
Rev. Canon William S. Van Meter
 Exec. Secy, Dept. Christian Social Relations, Protestant Council of City of N. Y.

SPONSORS
City Wide Committee for School Integration
 Rev. Milton Galamison, Chairman

Congress of Racial Equality
 James McCain, Dir. of Org.

Harlem Parents Committee
 Isaiah Robinson, Chairman

L. I. Coordinating Com. for Civil Rights
 Sidney Thompson, Chairman

Metropolitan Conf. for Civil Rights Action
 Rev. Edler G. Hawkins, Chairman

National Assoc. For the Advancement of Colored People
 Wm. C. Thompson, NYC Regional Dir.

National Assn. for Puerto Rican Civil Rights
 Gerena Valentin, Chairman

Urban League of Greater N. Y.
 Alexander J. Allen, Executive Director

Westchester Coordinating Committee For Justice Now
 Dr. John Codington
 Phillip Jenkins, Co-Chairmen

Dist. 65 R.WDSU AFL-CIO
 David Livingston, Pres.

Local 1199 (Drug & Hosp. Union) RWDSU AFL-CIO
 Leon Davis, Pres.

Local 485 IUE AFL-CIO
 Clifton Cameron, Business Mgr.

Local 259 UAW AFL-CIO
 Sam Meyers, Pres.

Local 237 City Emp. of IBT
 William Lewis, Pres.

Local 210 IBT
 Joe Konowe, Sec. Treas.

CO-ORDINATOR
Cleveland Robinson
 Secy-Treas., Dist. 65, AFL-CIO

Following the landmark March on Washington in August, 1963, national civil rights legislation was subject to the delaying tactics of segregationist southern senators, including endless speeches and debates referred to collectively as the filibuster. This deadlock led to another march on Washington, along with related lobbying and other political activities to exert pressure for Congressional action. An impressive coalition of civic, cultural, religious, labor, and educational groups organized the initiatives, which were peaceful, nonviolent, and well within the traditional boundaries of American politics.

Throughout 1965, there were a series of marches, demonstrations, and picketing at Jack London Square in Oakland, California, aimed at ending employment discrimination in restaurants and other businesses. This was the first step in a broader civil rights campaign that sought to address multiple issues by bringing protest tactics from the South to a northern city. CORE, the Congress of Racial Equality, was the lead organizer of these multi-racial activities, which included among their participants students from the University of California, Berkeley.

WHO WILL BE NEXT?

This morning, March 3, a young man was buried in Selma, Alabama after he died of a bullet wound inflicted by a state trooper. His name was James Lee Jackson and he came from a Negro family active in the local Movement to achieve equal voting rights.

This is the story: On the night of February 18, 1965, a group of about 300 people came out of a church where they had met to plan a march to the courthouse to demand the vote. State troopers were waiting. The people knelt to pray. The troopers began beating them with billy clubs. Many people were hospitalized; at least 10 men had broken scalps. Several hours later, Jimmy Jackson was in a cafe when troopers came in looking for someone who had allegedly thrown a Coca-Cola bottle at the troopers during the beating. They grabbed Jackson and shot him in the stomach. He ran out the door; troopers followed and beat him. He died the following week in a Selma hospital. His mother and grandfather, age 80, were also beaten on that terrible night.

BUT THERE WERE OTHERS BEFORE HIM; AMONG THEM:

Herbert Lee -- Negro voter registration worker killed in Liberty, Mississippi in 1961.

William Moore -- a white postman, shot to death in 1963 while on a one-man freedom walk urging an end to discrimination.

Medgar Evers -- N.A.A.C.P. leader in Mississippi, shot to death in 1963

Louis Allen -- Negro witness to Herbert Lee's murder, who was shotgunned to death in January, 1964 when he was about to tell the F.B.I. who had killed Lee.

Michael Schwerner --white C.O.R.E. worker for the Mississippi Summer Project shot to death in the town of Philadelphia, Miss. in 1964.

James Chaney -- Negro from Meridian, Miss., killed with Schwerner.

Andrew Goodman -- white volunteer worker from New York City, the third of the group killed in Philadelphia.

And now Jimmy Lee Jackson.

The government's recent promises of a new Voting Bill did not prevent him from being killed. We go on talking while men die. The brutality and killing will go on unless concrete action is taken now. Sheriff Jim Clark of Dallas County holds primary responsibility for the pattern of violence against Negroes in Alabama. He has violated federal laws again and again. If federal action is taken against him, the police may cease to beat innocent people, use electric cattle-prods on schoolchildren, and shoot down men like animals.
WIRE OR WRITE THE PRESIDENT, THE DEPARTMENT OF JUSTICE, OR YOUR CONGRESSMAN DEMANDING

SUCH ACTION NOW. URGE YOUR FRIENDS AND ASSOCIATES TO DO THE SAME. RUN ADVERTISEMENTS,

ORGANIZE PETITIONS, LET THE NATION HEAR YOU.

If you do, perhaps -- perhaps -- no one will be next.

Student Nonviolent Coordinating Committee
100 Fifth Avenue
New York, N.Y.

Violence and the palpable threat of violence cast a dark shadow over civil rights proponents throughout the period from the mid-1950s through the 1960s. The leaflet cites some tragic examples that occurred prior to President Lyndon Johnson signing the landmark Voting Rights Act on August 6, 1965. At this stage the emphasis was on pressuring elements of the federal government—the President, the Department of Justice, and Congress—to protect the rights and lives of all citizens, including those who were protesting nonviolently.

Where is Lowndes County?

Lowndes County is in the "Heart of Dixie." It is a county in Alabama, and its population is 80% black, while its government is 100% white. Although Negroes do most of the work in Lowndes, they have nothing to show for it. They own but a tiny portion of the land; they attend school in delapidated, overcrowded, and understaffed schools; and the roads in front of their homes are unpaved. In brief, they live under conditions of poverty, poor housing, over work, under pay, high taxation, with little hope for the future. This life is in striking contrast to the life of the white minority, which owns most of the land, has good jobs, has paved streets, and attends spacious, modern schools.

Lowndes is not a poor county. It has rich plantations, and the $30 million Dan River Textile Mill. The county government could easily eliminate all remnants of poverty, pave all roads, recondition all schools if it wanted to; but so far it has not seen fit to do so. One reason is that all large land holdings and the Dan River Mill goes untaxed; consequently, there is little money for government, and almost all this goes for the white community.

What is the L.C.F.O.?

For the first time since Reconstruction, the Negro in the South has the vote. But they reason that, "Having the vote without having a say as to who is running is as good as no vote at all." "Negroes in the North have the vote, but they're no better off than we are," they observe. So they have decided to start the Freedom Organization which they control, that they can call their own. For the first time these people have gotten together to form an organization that is truly democratic and responsive to their needs.

The Afro-American community of Lowndes County lives in constant fear. Fear of not having enough to eat. Fear of not having enough to wear. Fear of disease. Fear of not having a roof over one's head. And fear of police suppression if it tries to do anything about its problems.

But the black people have decided that things have to change. They are "sick and tired of being sick and tired." So they have formed the LOWNDES COUNTY FREEDOM ORGANIZATION in order to fight for political power -- the only way to change social conditions.

The L.C.F.O. means the beginnings of a new life for the people who live there. A new hope for a better future: better jobs, better schools, better neighborhoods, better lives! It means an over all feeling of dignity and self-respect.

The L.C.F.O. is a vitally encouraging example to all people, black and white. It is an example of "little people" getting together to solve their problems, to control their government, and hence control their own lives.

What is L.C.F.O. doing?

• **Registering Voters.** Two years ago there were no Negroes registered. Today after SNCC initiated a registration drive, the LCFO has registered over 2600 of the 5000 eligible Negroes. Even though over 130% of the whites are registered (!), Negroes still have the majority!

• **Running Candidates.** Negroes came together democratically to nominate candidates that would honestly represent them. The candidates are for: Sheriff, Tax Collector, Tax Assessor, Coroner, and three members of the Board of Education. These candidates are running on a program of tax reform, school reform, and general social-civic reform.

ONE MAN - ONE VOTE

Their symbol is the "Black Panther" which stands for courage, determination, and freedom. It was chosen as an appropriate response to the racist Alabama Democratic Party symbol, the white rooster and its slogan, "White Supremacy/ For the Right."

• **Health Clinics.** Over 90% of the children in the county are undernourished. Most of the adults suffer with high blood pressure. There is a high mortality rate among black people. LCFO is doing things for the people NOW! It is initiating a health campaign, and it is setting up a clinic with doctors and other medical staff.

The Lowndes County (Alabama) Freedom Organization—LCFO—was established in 1965 as a response to the dire living conditions and exclusion from political power that African Americans experienced in the county. The leaflet presents the history, agenda, and significance of the organization, and features the LCFO's symbol: a black panther, representing courage, determination, dignity, and empowerment. Distinct from the national Black Panther Party for Self-Defense founded in Oakland, California, in 1966, the LCFO was an independent alternative to the Whites-only Democratic Party in Alabama and supported candidates for public office in Lowndes County.

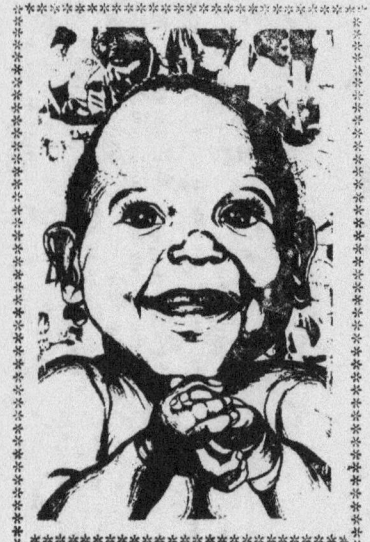

A PROGRAM FOR SURVIVAL

People's Free Food Program

Provides free food to Black and other oppressed people.

Free Busing to Prisons Program

Provides free transportation to prisons for families and friends of incarcerated men and women.

David Hilliard People's Free Shoe Program

Provides free shoes to the people made at the David Hilliard Free Shoe Factory and elsewhere.

Seniors Against A Fearful Environment (S.A.F.E.) Program

Provides free transportation and escort service for senior citizens to and from community banks the first of each month.

This is the list of the "programs" that the Detroit Branch is sponsoring but they can't be successful without the help from you, The People!

For further information contact---822-0835
2228 Bewick, Det. Br. Black Panther Party

Literature from the Black Panther Party offered distinctly mixed messages. The Party often portrayed itself as a revolutionary vanguard fighting for the liberation of oppressed African Americans against U.S. racism, capitalism, and imperialism. Panther language and terminology alluded to the possibility of responding violently to such systemic conditions without directly advocating specific acts. At the same time, the party expressed themes of Black self-empowerment as it offered support and assistance programs similar to those associated with traditional social-service organizations.

This "Free Huey" rally was held in 1968. Huey Newton and Bobby Seale had established the Black Panther Party for Self-Defense during October, 1966, in Oakland, California. The Party was a response to incidents of police brutality inflicted on African Americans. Panther members, dressed in black and carrying weapons, monitored police behavior. On October 28, 1967, Newton was arrested and imprisoned following a violent confrontation with Oakland police, during which an officer, John Frey, was killed. Huey's treatment by authorities led to the Free Huey campaign. Eventually, in 1970, all charges against Newton were dropped.

Dr. Martin Luther King lived and died in the pursuit of social and economic justice for all. His last months were spent in the development of a Poor Peoples' Campaign to confront the nation with the desperate problems of poor people of all races.

Martin Luther King's vision of the civil rights movement evolved beyond pushing for national legislation to combat historic discrimination and segregation. His efforts became more comprehensive, defining a broader set of civil rights related to the circumstances of impoverished, disadvantaged people from a broad range of ethnicities and cultures. The Poor Peoples' Campaign was an expression of that more inclusive agenda.

BLACK POWER

The concept of Black Power was first developed in Lowdes County, Alabama by SNCC in its struggle against the white racist power that ruled a county where 60% of the population was black, but where all the county officials were white, where there was no money for the black schools and only minimal taxation of the white-held farms and industries. Black Power here meant control of the county by its people. Black people wanted a decent life NOW -- they refused to wait until the gradual process of integration would absorb a tiny minority of black men into white society.

Black Power spread into the urban ghettos, where racism is less overt but nevertheless present. The slogan of "Black Power" was concretized into a program for black liberation which stated that black people must have economic and political control of their community--they must control the schools and police, and stop the economic exploitation of the ghetto by merchants and landlords as well as break from the two-party system and instead organize independent political organizations to articulate their demands.

The development from integration to Black Power was also a lesson for the white community. In the middle 60's many white college students had gone to jail and been beaten by police during the civil rights movement. In 1965 Stokeley Carmichael spoke at the Greek Theater of the University of California in Berkeley and defined the relationship between the white movement and Black Power. Carmichael called on white students to fight racism in its heartland--the white community. The job for white students, he said, was to build a movement in the white community while black people developed their own movement in the black community. These two movements could join together in a coalition based on mutual respect on those issues where the interests of the black and white struggles ran together.

At NYU we see the fruition of the coalition strategy in the struggle of BASA and the white strike committee to reinstate John Hatchett, the choice of the black student community as head of the Afro-American Student Center. Both black and white students have a vested interest in fighting the administration which so easily capitulates to outside pressures in determining its policy.

The demand is raised that black students and not the university administration must be the constituency to whom Hatchett is responsible--for he is the representative of the black students, and they must decide whether he is satisfying the requirements of the job. The second demand, for black control, is the same demand that black parents are raising at Ocean Hill-Brownsville and the Black Panthers are raising in the black communities. Because black people have historically been exploited in this society, they are organizing for control of their community.

The struggle for black liberation is a struggle for intellectual liberation as well as material liberation. It also means that black people must develop those forms of culture and expression which fit their needs and experiences. That is why it is important that the university have an institution such as the Afro-American Student Center, under the control of the black students and not the administration, so that black students can develop an alternative to the social structure which has oppressed them so long.

It is the responsibility of all of us, black and white, to struggle to control our lives and our universities. The administration is strong; if we do not struggle to achieve every aspect of that control, we have no hope of success.

STRIKE!

The concept of Black Power arose in response to two intertwined and deeply rooted conditions: White racism and Black powerlessness. While the leaflet concerns the fate of New York University's Afro-American Student Center (established in 1968), its broader focus is these two basic characteristics of American society. Black Power meant that Blacks must define and direct the struggle for liberation from political, economic, cultural, and psychological oppression through the process of exercising their own forms of leadership. The role of Whites is to be supportive of this approach and challenge White racism in all of its manifestations.

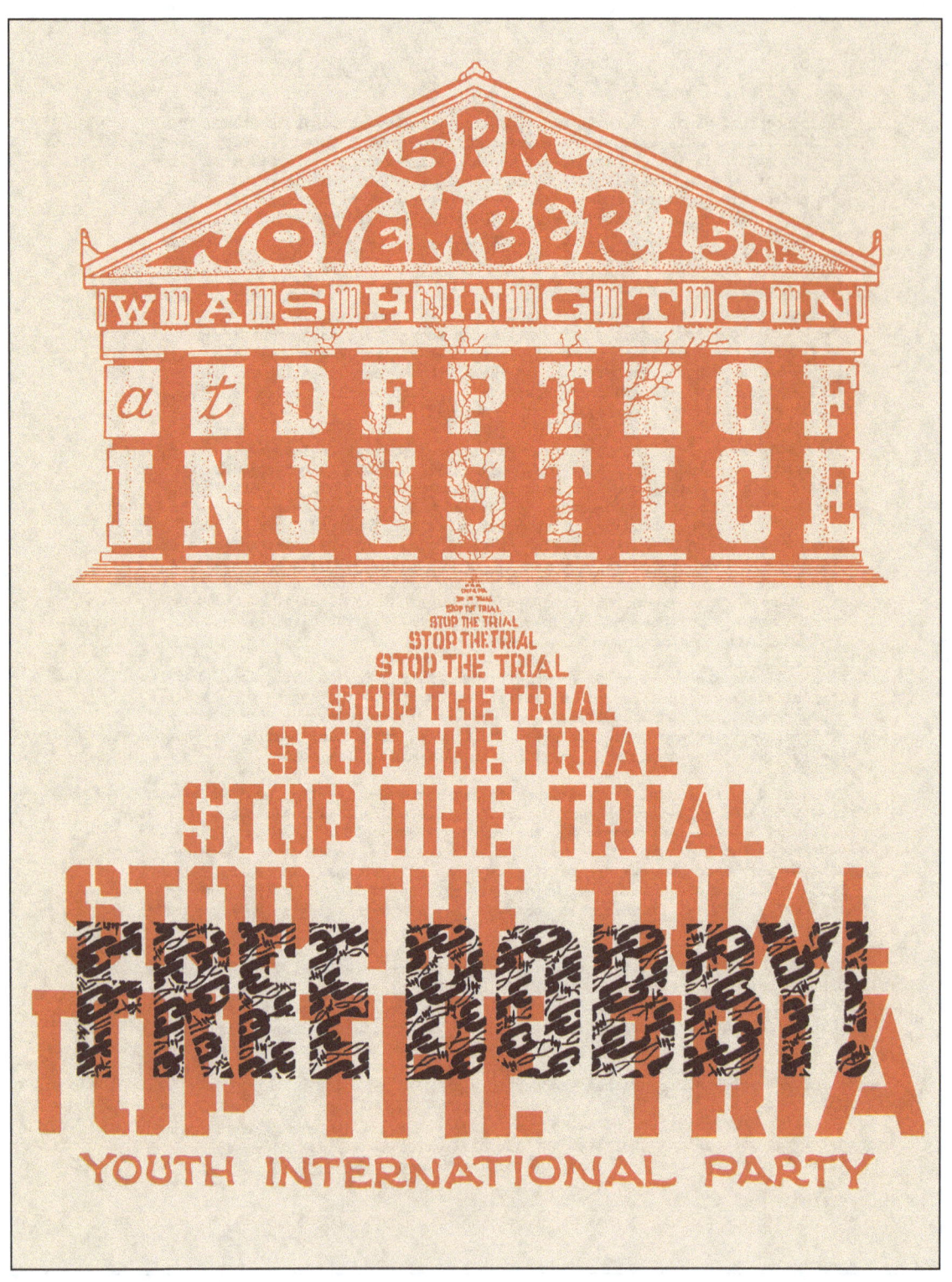

Following the tumultuous demonstrations in Chicago during the 1968 Democratic Convention, the federal government charged eight men with conspiracy to incite violence, including Bobby Seale, a founder of the Black Panthers. The trial began in the fall of 1969. Seale objected when Judge Julius Hoffman refused his request to represent himself; he was then bound, gagged, and chained to a chair in the courtroom. Seale's case ended in a mistrial and was never re-tried; convictions of the other defendants were overturned in 1972. (The Youth International Party—"Yippies"—was a group of radicals whose street-theater tactics expressed their disdain for conventional political processes.)

COPS OUT OF VIETNAM
COPS OUT OF THE GHETTO

STOP THE DRAFT WEEK
APRIL 23

OAKLAND INDUCTION CENTER
6:30 - 9:30

ALAMEDA COUNTY COURTHOUSE
10:00 - noon

The twin figures of a soldier and a policeman symbolize the conviction that both were occupying forces engaged in the oppression of non-White populations at home and abroad. Identifying racism and imperialism as two sides of the same coin was intended to unite anti-war activists with those who were active in the movements for civil rights and Black Power. "Stop the Draft Week" 1968 was an effort to disrupt the processing of military recruits in Oakland, California.

SHOW SOLIDARITY
with
BLACK REBELLION in New Jersey

RALLY

Friday · Noon · Sproul

DEMONSTRATION - MONDAY
Oakland Courthouse - 12:00
· 12th & Fallon ·
carpools - 11:00 am - Bancroft
+
Dana

What happened:

A Black Rebellion has been going on for 3 days in Ashbury
Park, New Jersey. Thousands are battling the cops around
demands for more jobs, better housing and a fence around
the railroad tracks. (It seems the side of the tracks
facing the black community has no fence and children have
been killed and injured there. The side facing the white
community has a fence.)
At least 200 people have been arrested, 14 are hospitalized.
The cops have sealed off 25 blocks of the city. Last night
the cops opened fire on a crowd, wounding 45. This repression
must stop. We demand : all arrested be freed - cops out
of the community.

SDS

FIGHT RACISM + REPRESSION

Asbury Park, a coastal community in Monmouth County, New Jersey, experienced major unrest and violence in early July, 1970. Local Black residents were frustrated and resentful over historic grievances involving deprivation, poverty, housing discrimination, lack of employment opportunities, and abusive treatment by police. According to news reports, youth congregating at a July 4 dance became unruly; police responded, followed by escalating confrontations over the next few days. The leaflet is attributed to SDS—Students for a Democratic Society—although by 1970 that organization had splintered into conflicting factions.

People's No. 1 Enemy

Definition of a PIG:

A LOW NATURED BEAST, THAT HAS
NO REGARD FOR LAW OR JUSTICE;
OR THE RIGHTS OF THE PEOPLE.
BITES THE HAND THAT FEEDS IT;
USUALLY MASQUERADING AS THE
VICTIM OF AN UNPROVOKED ATTACK!

PEOPLE BEWARE! Pigs come in all colors — from a white racist to the blackest of lackeys — all Kill!

Our Minister of Defense, HUEY P. NEWTON says:

"AN UNARMED PEOPLE ARE SLAVES, OR ARE SUBJECT TO SLAVERY AT ANY GIVEN MOMENT!---The racist dog oppressor fears the armed people; they fear most of all Black people armed with weapons and the ideology of the BLACK PANTHER PARTY! Black people are held captive in the midst of their oppressor---there is a world of difference between thirty million unarmed submissive Black people. and thirty million Black people armed with freedom and defense guns and the strategic methods of liberation!"

THE RACIST DOG POLICEMAN MUST WITHDRAW IMMEDIATELY FROM OUR COMMUNITIES, CEASE THEIR WANTON MURDER AND BRUTALITY AND TORTURE OF BLACK PEOPLE....

— or —

---- FACE THE WRATH OF THE ARMED PEOPLE!!!

WHEN A MECHANIC WANTS TO FIX A BROKEN CAR ENGINE, HE NEEDS THE NECESSARY TOOLS-----WHEN THE PEOPLE MOVE FOR LIBERATION, THEY MUST HAVE THE BASIC TOOL OF LIBERATION---THEY MUST HAVE THE GUN!!!

Philadelphia Branch
of the B.P.P.
1928 Columbia Avenue
N. Philadelphia, Pa. 19121

"Pig" was a derisive name used by activists for police, both White and Black. The position of the Black Panther Party, stated here, was that Black people were imprisoned and victimized in their communities by police forces, and therefore possession of guns was necessary for self-defense. The language represents the ownership of weapons as symbolizing freedom and liberation from oppression, but is careful not to explicitly advocate their use.

APRIL 23
STOP THE DRAFT WEEK

Oakland Induction Center
Alameda County Courthouse

U.S. imperialism at home and abroad has not changed. Even if the war in Vietnam is ended, our government will continue to deny the right to self-determination to the world's people. Black people in this country are oppressed politically and economically. Leaders of the black liberation struggle are being murdered and jailed. To bring about real changes in this country, we must keep our movement strong, militant, and in the streets. Join us April 23.

- **Withdraw troops from Vietnam**
- **Get the cops out of the ghetto**
- **Free Huey Newton**
- **End the draft**
- **Black control of the black community**

"Stop the Draft Week" in 1968 was a series of anti-war demonstrations culminating in an attempt to disrupt the processing of young men for military service at the Oakland, California Induction Center. The leaflet, though, speaks of "U.S. imperialism at home and abroad" as being a broader protest target. It affirms "the right to self-determination" for those who are "oppressed politically and economically," and encompasses "the Black liberation struggle" as well. The call to withdraw troops from Vietnam and remove cops from the ghetto was a challenge to U.S. imperialism both internationally and domestically.

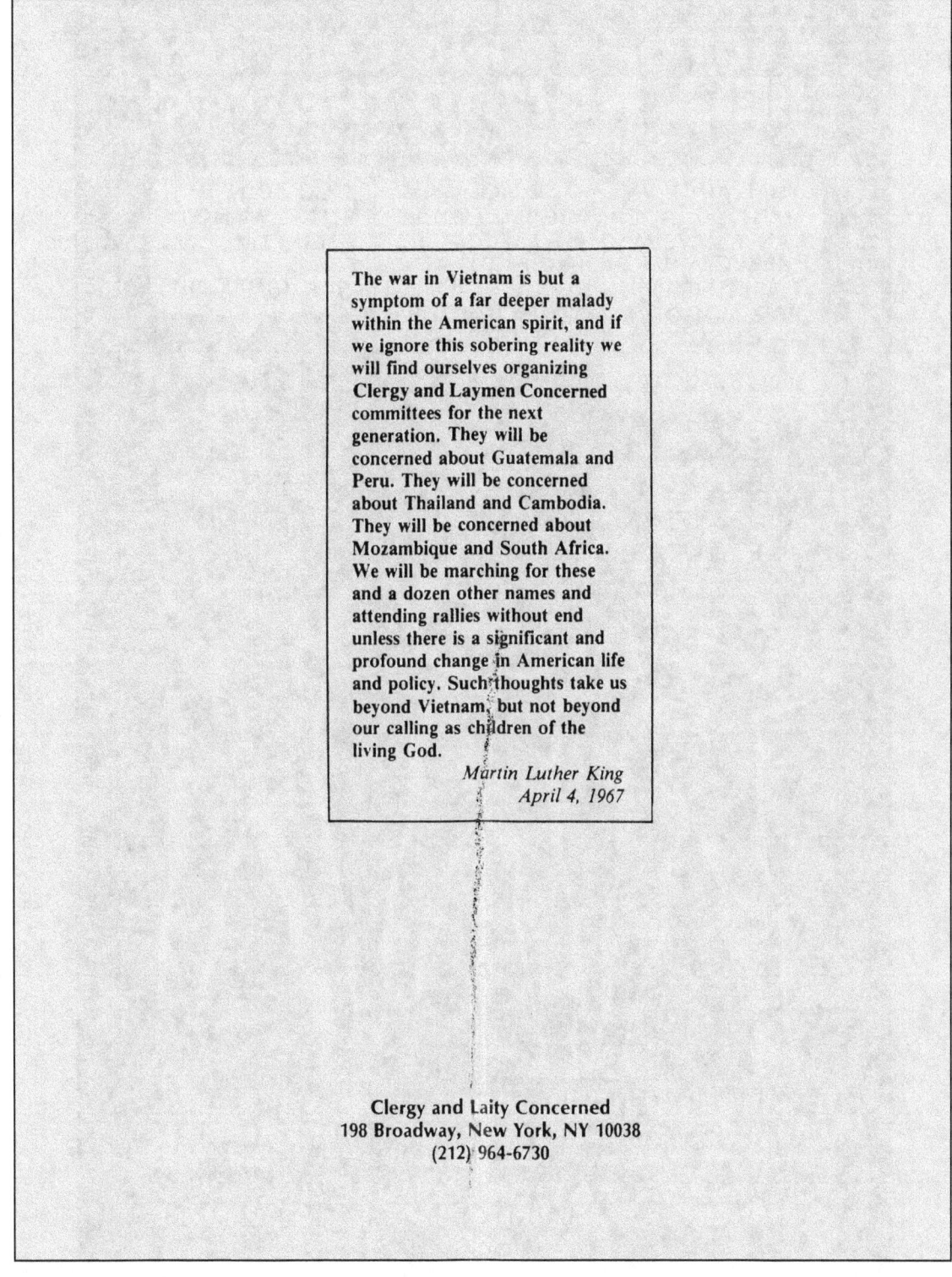

The war in Vietnam is but a symptom of a far deeper malady within the American spirit, and if we ignore this sobering reality we will find ourselves organizing Clergy and Laymen Concerned committees for the next generation. They will be concerned about Guatemala and Peru. They will be concerned about Thailand and Cambodia. They will be concerned about Mozambique and South Africa. We will be marching for these and a dozen other names and attending rallies without end unless there is a significant and profound change in American life and policy. Such thoughts take us beyond Vietnam, but not beyond our calling as children of the living God.

Martin Luther King
April 4, 1967

Clergy and Laity Concerned
198 Broadway, New York, NY 10038
(212) 964-6730

After much thought and reflection involving considerations of morality, religious conviction, and political strategy, Rev. Martin Luther King Jr. spoke out strongly against U.S. military involvement in Vietnam. King's speech at Riverside Church in New York City on April 4, 1967, in effect joined the civil rights and anti-war movements under a common message that our presence in Vietnam was an unjustified invasion, weakening the United States by diverting resources that could be used to meet domestic needs such as fighting poverty, alleviating unemployment, and improving education. Exactly one year later, King was assassinated.

Different ways to resist fighting in Vietnam are portrayed with a special focus on communicating with young African American men about their options regarding being drafted into military service. The interlocked arms of the three figures indicate that Black men should support each other by refusing to become combatants in Vietnam—in other words, by forging an Alliance for Black Unity.

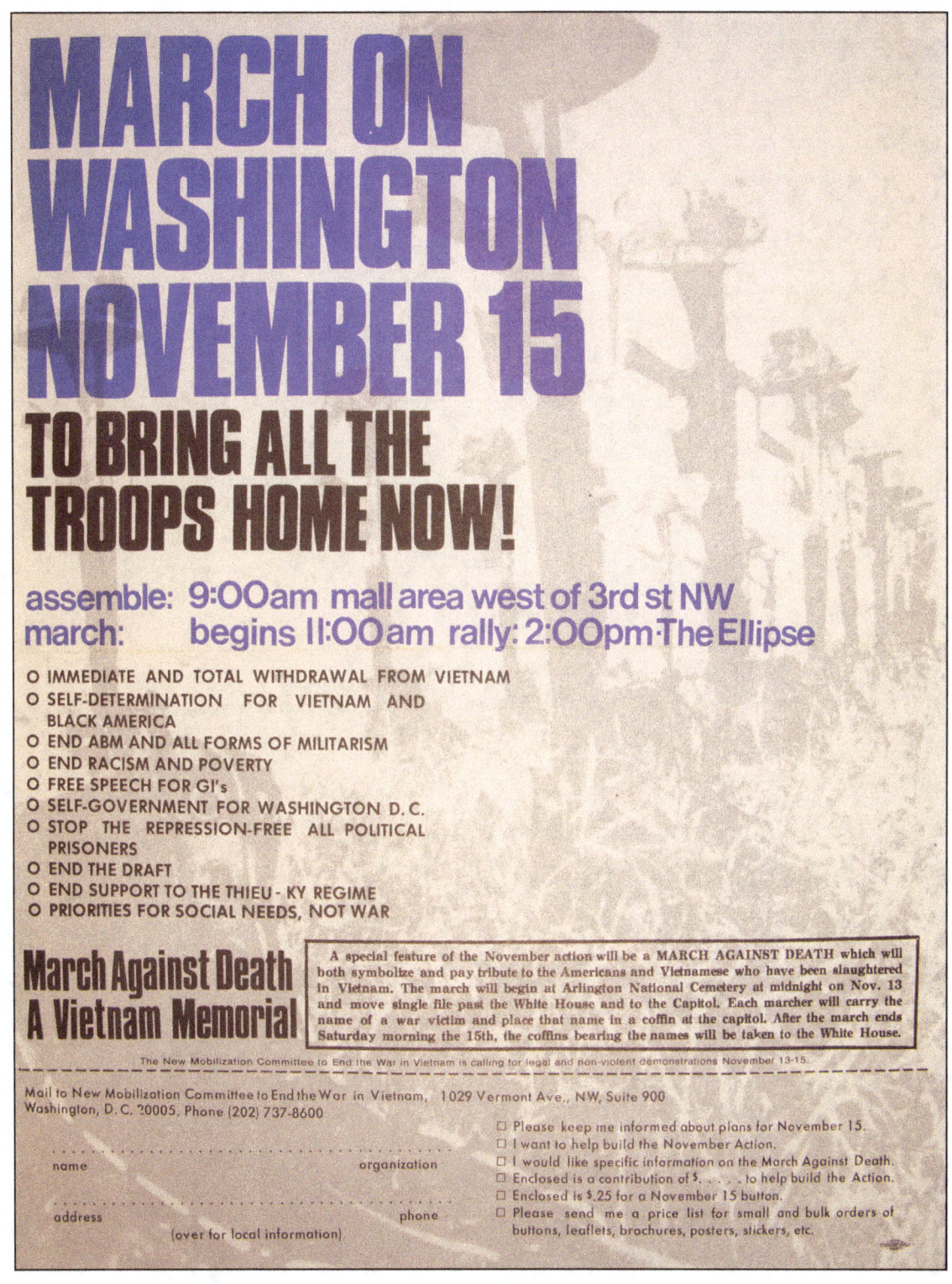

As part of a nationwide initiative orchestrated by the New Mobilization Committee to End the War in Vietnam, in excess of 500,000 people gathered in Washington, D.C., on November 15, 1969. Organizers wanted to attract protesters across a broad spectrum, so the event emphasized a multitude of connected issues and priorities including civil rights, Black Power, racism, poverty, the draft, and equal justice, and called for re-directing resources from war to domestic development. ("ABM" is the anti-ballistic missile system; "Thieu-Ky regime" refers to the government of South Vietnam.)

SECTION 2

Opposition to the War in Vietnam

"THE ANTI-WAR MOVEMENT" is a commonly used phrase in discussions of the Sixties when referring to protests against American military intervention in Vietnam. It is convenient as a kind of historical shorthand but in actuality is quite misleading and conveys the impression of a singular, coherent, uniform entity. This is an example of how the understandable tendency to compress or reduce multi-dimensional phenomena into simplistic terminology diminishes their dynamism and vitality.

Indeed, one of the most noteworthy aspects of the anti-war movement was the extremely wide diversity of its participants, whose motivations covered a spectrum ranging from religious or philosophical pacifism to virulent rejection of American capitalism and imperialism. A broad desire to see an end to U.S. involvement in the Vietnamese civil war did, on a general level, unite those various participants. Differences in perspective and motivation, however, were manifested in the frequent debates and conflicts over ideology, strategy, and organizational structure within and between the disparate groups and factions that comprised the anti-war movement as a whole.

The leaflets in this section reflect some of the numerous viewpoints and actions that constituted the anti-war movement of the Sixties. In so doing, they reveal the many ways in which Americans protested their government's actions in Vietnam.

Objections to the draft, military conscription, and the Selective Service System are a major category of anti-war leaflets. They illustrate the varieties of anti-draft efforts, such as counseling to avoid or evade the draft, refusing induction, obstructing the operations of an induction center, burning or turning in draft cards, and total non-cooperation with Selective Service processes. The anti-draft leaflets reveal the contrast and tension within this segment of the anti-war movement between individual acts of conscience as exemplified by the Resistance and disruptive group actions such as "Stop the Draft Week" demonstrations.

No group opposed the draft so completely, so unconditionally, so uncompromisingly as the Resistance. Resistance members deliberately and consciously chose bold forms of civil disobedience. They refused to obey the directives of the Selective Service System, burned or returned their draft registration cards, did not submit to being inducted into the military, and consequently in some cases went to jail.

Participants in the Resistance viewed the draft as one part of a larger network of physical and psychological oppression, which they were determined to expose and confront. They saw a connection between denying the legitimacy of the draft; ending U.S. involvement in Vietnam; reducing the national and international influence of the U.S. military-industrial complex; and building democratic, humanly scaled communities. The Resistance was a unique blend of philosophy, morality, and spirituality manifested in an intensely personal form of political expression.

The Resistance emphasized individuals "bearing witness" as being more important than joining large protest activities. This meant acting on the basis of moral principles and beliefs, serving as an example for others to do the same. The Resistance viewed itself as a community of "brothers and sisters" rather than a structured organization. Finally, the Resistance considered refusal to cooperate with the Selective Service System, which required a very high level of commitment, to be the most direct challenge possible to government war-making authority.

Other people in the anti-war movement believed that the tactics and rationale of the Resistance were futile at best and self-indulgent at worst. After all, some argued, how effectively can you oppose the Vietnam War if you are in jail? Wouldn't the government prefer to have you there instead of out in the streets marching? Rather than being against the draft on your own, come together with others to interrupt and disrupt the processing operations of military induction centers through militant demonstrations. This viewpoint is found in a stop-the-draft leaflet featuring the slogan, "Hell no, nobody goes!" "The time has come for individuals to stop talking about resisting," it proclaimed, instead urging "collective political action against the draft . . . by doing all we can to shut down the Oakland [California] Induction Center."

Another category of anti-war leaflets concerns soldiers who objected to fighting in Vietnam and the struggle, as one leaflet put it, "To win a Bill of Rights for rank-and-file servicemen and women." There are also leaflets promoting protest actions at specific military bases and installations.

Specialized forms of opposition against particular facets of America's war effort can be distinguished from large marches and rallies that were oriented along general themes such as withdrawing all U.S. troops from Vietnam. The former sought to focus dissent on identifiable activities either directly or indirectly linked to American military intervention. Thus, there are leaflets that are more targeted in their message, audience, and activity. For instance, halting a troop train carrying soldiers; a campaign to stop the manufacture of napalm; a vigil at a munitions depot; and boycotts of products from the Dow Chemical Company in reaction to its involvement with making napalm.

Anti-war leaflets with women's concerns and issues as their core content (included in this section and in the Women's Liberation section) emphasize the profound awakening of feminist consciousness as one of the principal cultural developments to emerge out of the anti-war movement. Dissatisfaction with their role and status in the anti-war movement was acutely experienced by women, who did not hesitate to point out the sexist behavior directed toward them by supposedly enlightened, progressive men. This hypocrisy fueled the emergence and assertion of women's initiatives in response to oppression both in the anti-war movement and throughout American society as a whole. Women began to believe that it was necessary to break away from male-dominated groups and to organize by and for themselves in order to genuinely redefine their social, cultural, and sexual identities free from the influence of domineering men.

Opposition to American intervention in Vietnam was viewed by some as connected to other issues and policies that contributed to, or were influenced by, that involvement: the draft, weapons production, poverty, inequality, discrimination, injustice, urban decay, ecological devastation, and powerlessness. The combination of the civil rights and anti-war movements provided the impetus for a widespread, penetrating examination of American society. As a result, nationalism, militarism, imperialism, racism, sexism, elitism, and materialism all came under scrutiny. Some leaflets in this section thus link protesting the Vietnam War to a broader political, economic, and cultural agenda that addressed a range of related problems.

During the Sixties, there were different but concurrent kinds of anti-war activism, depending on the motivations, beliefs, and commitment level of participating individuals and organizations. Many directions and orientations, and derivations thereof, constituted the opposition to American intervention in Vietnam, as the leaflets in this section exemplify.

One of the great strengths of the Vietnam War protest movement was that an immense variety of divergent perspectives coalesced under the anti-war banner. It was also, paradoxically, one of the movement's profound weaknesses, producing a wide but thin unity that was periodically threatened by the stresses and strains of its own differences.

STOP
the
TROOP TRAIN!

Another troop train is coming through Berkeley taking American boys to Vietnam to kill and be killed in a country where the U.S. does not belong.

We must demonstrate against the war machine; we must stop the train and give our anti-war literature tothe soldiers. To oppose the immoral war in Vietnam and to block the war machine is immoral; to take orders from an immoral state is immoral. The police will be on hand to try to help the war machine go through--without a second's stop. We will be there too.

We are not demonstrating against the soldiers. We consider the soldiers to be our brothers--brothers who have been conscripted against their will and forced to kill by a government which has forgotten how to tell the truth. We want to stop the war machine and tell the soldiers what is really going on in Vietnam.

thursday, august 12

SANTA FE STATION, BERKELEY 1300 University Ave:

TENTATIVE TIME: 8:45a.m.

For the exact arrival time call the Vietnam Day Committee Wednesday night, or come over to the office for further information.

2407 Fulton St., Berkeley   549-0811   or 845-6637

Car pools will be leaving for the Santa Fe Station at approximately 8 a.m. from the corner of Bancroft and Dana.

In early demonstrations against the Vietnam War, people attempted to block trains carrying soldiers by sitting down on the train tracks. It was the immorality of "the war machine" that motivated some to engage in such a direct and dangerous form of confrontation. This particular action took place in 1965.

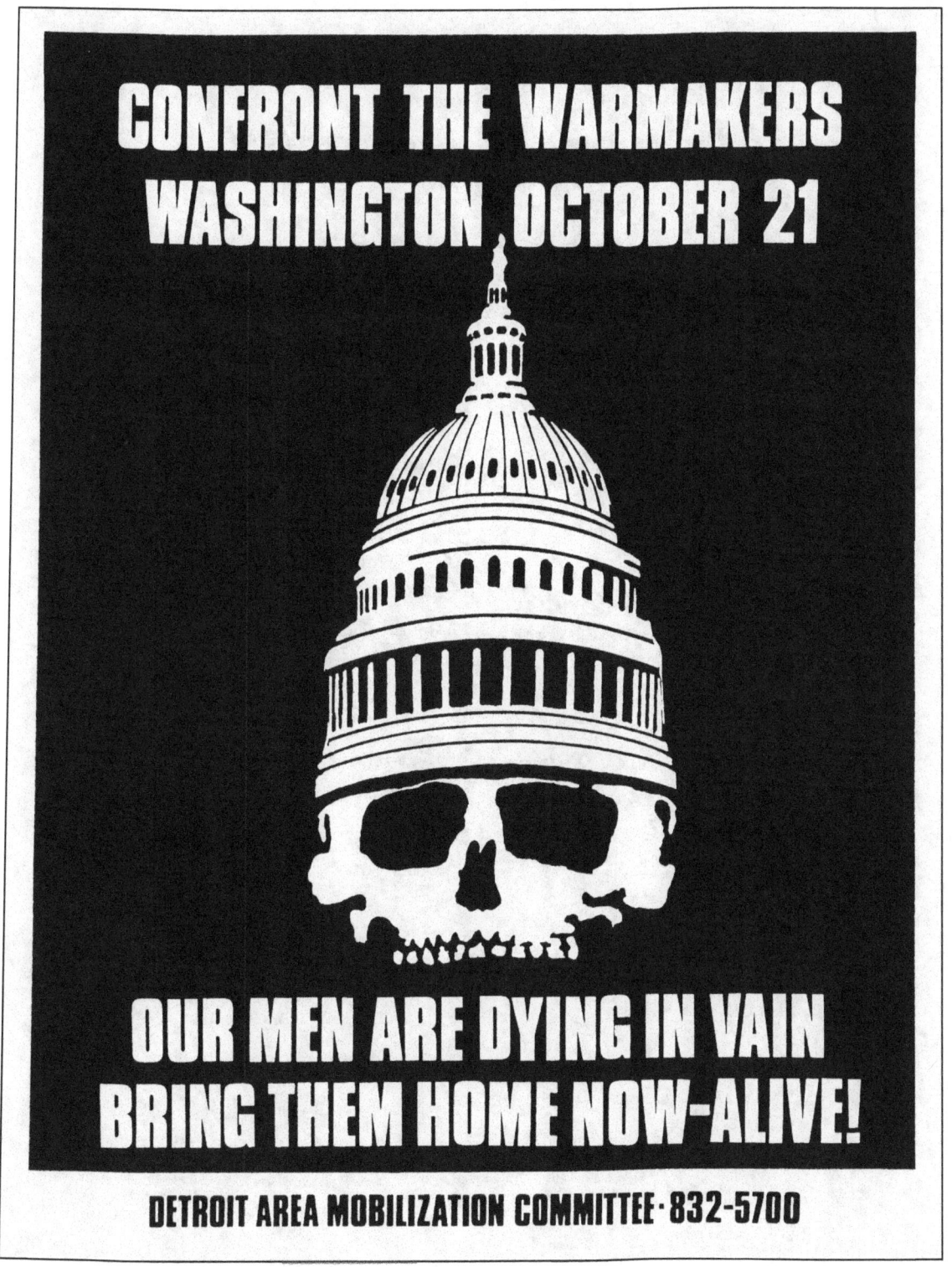

A simple, stark message, combined with a powerful graphic element, creates a leaflet with strong impact. Additional text would detract from that impact.

Vietnam Day Committee

tentative program for OCTOBER 15th & 16th

International Days of Protest

at Berkeley Campus & Oakland Army Terminal

Activities

FRIDAY - OCT. 15th

BERKELEY CAMPUS

9 - 12 am: Folksingers in upper Sproul Plaza. Discussion with speakers.

12 - 3 pm: Paul Goodman and others.

3 - 6 pm: Discussions on Vietnam and other workshop activities with speakers. Movies, folksinging, picnic supper.

6 - 7:30 pm: Pre-march Rally

7:30 - 11 pm:

Torchlight Peace March

with Loud-Speakers - Music - Banners!

11 - 12 pm: Rally at Army Base.

SATURDAY - OCT. 16th

OAKLAND ARMY TERMINAL

12:30 - 9 am: Army Base Sleep-out. Movies all night, folksingers, campfires, discussions and more discussions.

9 - 12 am: Workshops on: After Oct. 15 & 16 - next steps - Should VDC and other groups oppose Cohelan with a candidate? Another International Day of Protest? WHAT IF HANOI IS BOMBED?

12 - 5 pm: Final Speakers.

: ART & PHOTOGRAPH SHOW :

movies include-----
Hiroshima Mon Amour
I Live in Fear
Night and Fog
Hitler's Executioners

Speakers INCLUDE:

Fanny Lou Hamer - Mississippi Freedom Democratic Party

Paul Krassner - Editor of The Realist

Allen Ginsberg

Dave Dellinger - Editor of Liberation; Co-chairman of NYC Oct. 16 march

Paul Goodman - Author of Growing Up Absurd, The Empire City, etc.

Staughton Lynd

Marcus Raskin - Ex-aide to J. F. K.

"The Committee" - S. F. satirical group

Robert Scheer - Associate editor of Ramparts; just back from Saigon

Mike Myerson - Just back from Hanoi

A. J. Muste - C. N. V. A.

Hugh Hester - Brig. General, retired

Lawrence Ferlinghetti

Franz Schurmann - Faculty Peace Comm.

Donna Allen - Women for Peace

Bill Stanton - State Assemblyman

M. S. Arnoni - Editor of Minority of One

Stanley Sheinbuam - Ex-advisor to Diem

Paul Jacobs - Labor leader

Prof. Robert Browne - Ex-State Dept. official; just back from Saigon

Prof. Marshall Windmiller

Mark Spoelstra
Fugs - Joe McDonald
FOLKSINGERS

In August, 1965, the Berkeley Vietnam Day Committee, in conjunction with the National Coordinating Committee to End the War in Vietnam, designated October 15 and 16 as the International Days of Protest. In Berkeley, the International Days of Protest merged political activities with cultural ones. The structure of this eclectic event reflects a common pattern that coursed through the Sixties—the co-existence of two distinct but often overlapping arenas of rebellion. One emphasized political organizing, action, and commitment, and the other focused on a counterculture that explored and experimented with alternative lifestyles.

MARCH
ON WASHINGTON

In the name of freedom, America is mutilating Vietnam. In the name of peace, America turns that fertile country into a wasteland. And in the name of democracy, America is burying its own dreams and suffocating its own potential.

Americans who can understand why the Negroes of Watts can rebel should understand too why Vietnamese can rebel. And those who know the American South and the grinding poverty of our Northern cities should understand that our real problems lie not in Vietnam but at home — that the fight we seek is not with Communism but with the social desperation that makes good men violent, both here and abroad.

THE WAR MUST BE STOPPED

Our aim in Vietnam is the same as our aim in the United States: that oligarchic rule and privileged power be replaced by popular democracy where the people make the decisions which affect their lives and share in the abundance and opportunity that modern technology makes possible. This is the only solution for Vietnam in which Americans can find honor and take pride. Perhaps the war has already so embittered and devastated the Vietnamese that that ideal will require years of rebuilding. But the war cannot achieve it, nor can American military presence, nor our support of repressive unrepresentative governments.

The war must be stopped. There must be an immediate cease fire and demobilization in South Vietnam. There must be a withdrawal of American troops. Political amnesty must be guaranteed. All agreements must be ratified by the partisans of the "other side" — the National Liberation Front and North Vietnam.

We must not deceive ourselves: a negotiated agreement cannot **guarantee** democracy. Only the Vietnamese have the right of nationhood to make their government democratic or not, free or not, neutral or not. It is not America's role to deny them the chance to be what they will make of themselves. **That chance grows more remote with every American bomb that explodes in a Vietnamese village.**

But our hopes extend not only to Vietnam. Our chance is the first in a generation to organize the powerless and the voiceless at home to confront America with its racial injustice, its apathy, and its poverty, and with that same vision we dream for Vietnam: a vision of a society in which all can control their own destinies.

We are convinced that the only way to stop this and future wars is to organize a domestic social movement which challenges the very legitimacy of our foreign policy; this movement must also fight to end racism, to end the paternalism of our welfare system, to guarantee decent incomes for all, and to supplant the authoritarian control of our universities with a community of scholars.

This movement showed its potential when 25,000 people — students, the poverty-stricken, ministers, faculty, unionists, and others — marched on Washington last April. This movement must now show its force. SDS urges everyone who believes that our warmaking must be ended and our democracy-building must begin, **to join in a March on Washington on November 27, at 11 a.m. in front of the White House.**

Issued by: Students for a Democratic Society, 1103 East 63rd Street, Chicago—Phone: 667-6050

360

In 1965, two marches in Washington, D.C., on April 17 and November 27, moved opposition to the Vietnam War to the national stage. This leaflet, prepared by Students for a Democratic Society, was for the latter event. SDS, established in 1962, was a prominent activist organization during the Sixties, whose perspective saw domestic problems and conditions as being directly connected with American military intervention in Vietnam. The leaflet is a good example of that deeply critical and penetrating perspective.

Why We March Against the War in Vietnam

Every day young Americans are dying in a war that they don't understand. They say: I don't know the exact reasons for this war, but I've got to fight for the people back home. And the people back home say: I don't know what the war is really about, but our boys are over there and we've got to back them up.

It is a nightmare in which a small country is being bombed and machine-gunned into a mass of homeless refugees — all in the name of patriotism and anti-Communism. American foreign policy is more and more dominated by militarism and great-power arrogance. President Johnson talks about defending freedom and democracy in South Vietnam, but he knows as well as we do that we are defending the regime of General Nguyen Cao Ky, a military dictator of the worst sort, a small-time Hitler. ("People ask me who my heroes are. I have only one — Hitler." General Ky, interviewed in the London Sunday Mirror, July 4, 1965.)

What do you do when your country drifts into a war like this? If you don't care about America you say: "What business is it of mine?" or "I'll leave it to the President — he knows best." But if you are ashamed that America is acting like an international bully, if you are horrified when American boys are killed and maimed for no reason, then you want to stop this war.

A year ago, most Americans voted for Lyndon Johnson because he said he would be cautious in Vietnam. But Johnson thought that the American people had given him a blank check on election day; and since then he has gone on a wild spending spree of blood and money — our blood and money.

There are American soldiers who are dying today because they think we want them to. If we kept silent, we would be disloyal to them. We march against this war because we believe that our loyalty to humanity and to our country is far more important than any loyalty to politicians or generals.

SATURDAY, Nov. 20

March leaves 10AM from the Cal Campus (Bancroft & Telegraph)
ROUTE: Bancroft to Shattuck to Adeline ⟶ to DeFremery Park
Vietnam Day Committee, 2407 Fulton St., Berkeley, Calif., phone 549-0811

This 1965 announcement for a protest march reflects serious disenchantment with President Lyndon Johnson's deployment of troops to Vietnam barely a year after he defeated Republican Barry Goldwater in the 1964 presidential election. It argues that it is not disloyal or unpatriotic to question the Johnson Administration's Vietnam policy. Rather, in a country that proclaims the importance of freedom and democracy, it is our responsibility not to blindly believe what government officials say, especially regarding issues that involve life-and-death decisions.

All Troops
Home NOW!

MARCH & RALLY
OCTOBER 31
San Francisco

Assemble at 11am at Dolores Park, 18th and Dolores/Oct.31st Coalition, 922 Valencia St., San Francisco/282-8160/Vote for Peace Referendum on Nov. 3

The impression of a unified anti–war movement portrayed visually by a group of people marching under a common slogan was more hopeful than realistic. Participants may have agreed with a general demand—"All Troops Home NOW !"—for example, but their reasons for protesting ranged across a spectrum from pacifism to anti-imperialism, and encompassed a variety of beliefs, including that our intervention in Vietnam was immoral, illegal, racist, unwise, impractical, unwinnable, and costly.

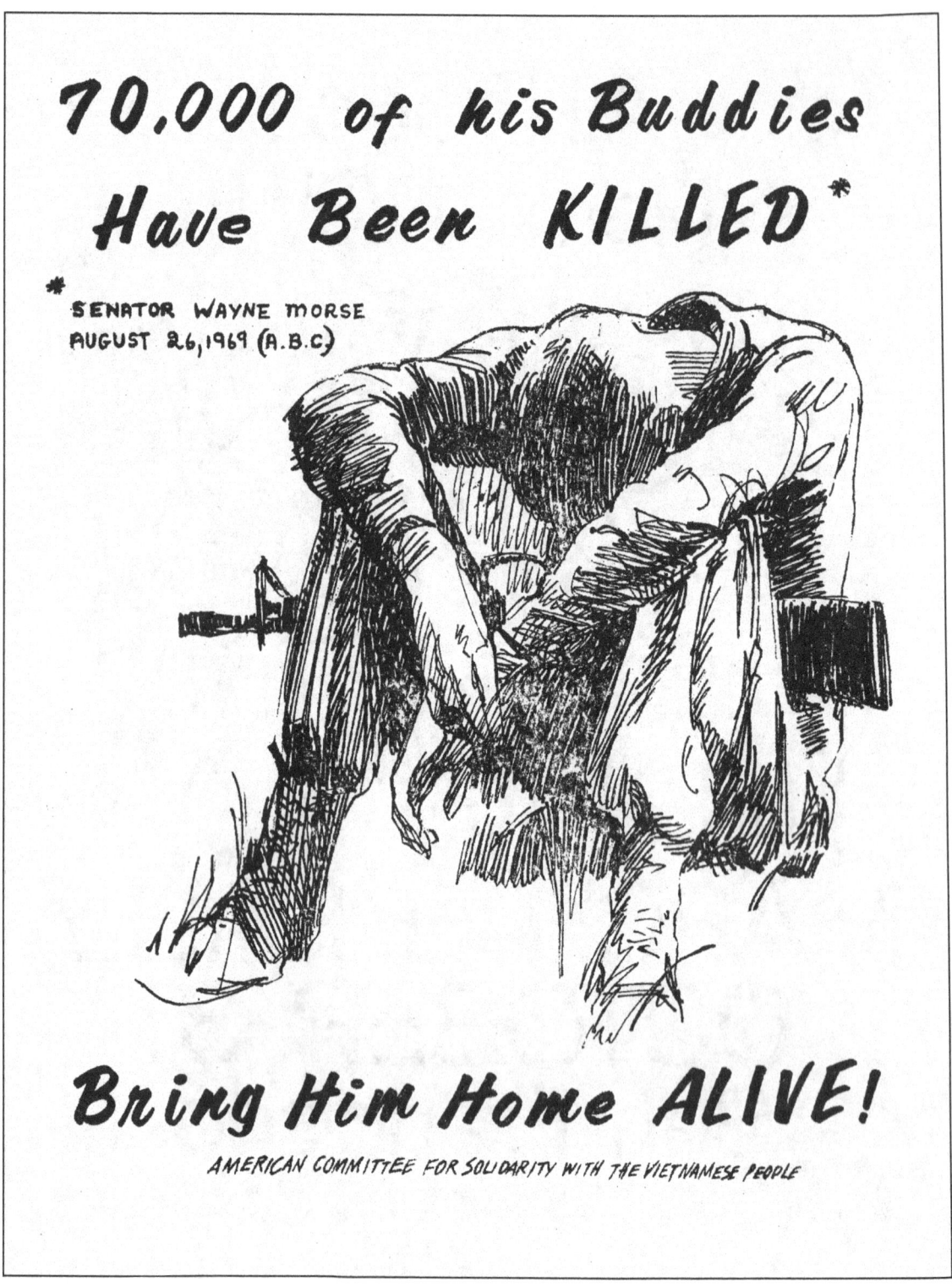

70,000 of his Buddies
Have Been KILLED*

* SENATOR WAYNE MORSE
AUGUST 26, 1969 (A.B.C.)

Bring Him Home ALIVE!

AMERICAN COMMITTEE FOR SOLIDARITY WITH THE VIETNAMESE PEOPLE

A tired and dejected U.S. soldier sits beneath a shocking message about how many like him have lost their lives in Vietnam. While the leaflet is from the American Committee For Solidarity with the Vietnamese People, it is focused on American deaths and the need to get our service members "home alive." The leaflet's anti-war message is, in a sense, both patriotic and nationalistic with its emphasis on U.S. casualties. What must be remembered is that America's intervention in Vietnam also resulted in an enormous death toll among Vietnamese civilians as well as Vietnamese military members, while American civilians were completely spared.

In 1969, the New Mobilization Committee to End the War in Vietnam organized two anti-war gatherings for the weekend following Veterans Day. Both events attracted large numbers of protesters—upwards of a quarter of a million in Washington, D.C., and an estimated 125,000 in San Francisco. Revolutionary Youth Movement – 2 / S.D.S., the group that produced this particular call for participation, was one of the three factions that emerged when Students for a Democratic Society fractured in June of 1969 during what turned out to be its final national conference.

**HELL NO
NOBODY GOES**

**HELL NO
NOBODY GOES**

**HELL NO
NOBODY GOES**

**HELL NO
NOBODY GOES**

**HELL NO
NOBODY GOES**

**HELL NO
NOBODY GOES**

**HELL NO
NOBODY GOES**

ORGANIZE

Lots of people have been saying they won't serve in Vietnam. It's not that easy. If you don't go, it's five years in jail. If you try to outwit the Army on your own, you usually end up with an induction notice. The time has come for individuals to stop talking about resisting -- they have to organize so they can resist effectively. Trained counselling and collective demonstrations make for 1-Y's and any of the other 12 deferments which can keep you out of the Army and out of jail.

STOP THE DRAFT
OCTOBER 16 - 21

Stop the Draft Week is a collective political action against the draft. We are going to exercise our power by doing all we can to shut down the Oakland Induction Center. In so doing, we will protest the basic premises of American foreign policy which lead to Vietnams. The draft is an indispensable tool used by the American system to oppress and control people in foreign countries. This anti-draft action will inform high school students, college students, and young working men that an anti-draft, anti-war movement exists which can help them and which will put its body on the line to save lives -- American and Vietnamese. Our aim is to give men the knowledge and the backing with which to combat the draft. We hope that through a public action against the draft young people on campus and off will band together permanently in draft unions to support each other when they say HELL NO -- WE WON'T GO! We believe that to permanently end the draft for war like Vietnam fundamental changes will have to be made in American society.

MEETINGS

Noon Rally, Sproul Steps, Wed. Oct. 4,
Noon Rally, Sproul Steps, Mon. Oct. 9,
    with Don Duncan, ex-Green Beret now with Ramparts
Meeting, Campus Stop the Draft Week Committee,
    Thursday, Oct. 5, Wesley Fndn., Bancroft & Dana,
    7:30 p.m.
Rally, DeFremery Park, Mon.,Oct. 16, 8 p.m.
    18th and Adeline Streets, Oakland
Party, Sat., Oct. 7, 1300 Arch St., 75¢

In 1967, Stop the Draft Week was organized as a week-long series of confrontations aimed at disrupting the operation of the Oakland, California, Induction Center and temporarily halting the drafting of young men into the military to serve in Vietnam. It was intended to express militant opposition to the war, climaxing with thousands of people filling the streets of downtown Oakland in an effort to shut down the induction center. Similar Stop the Draft Week demonstrations took place in several cities around the country.

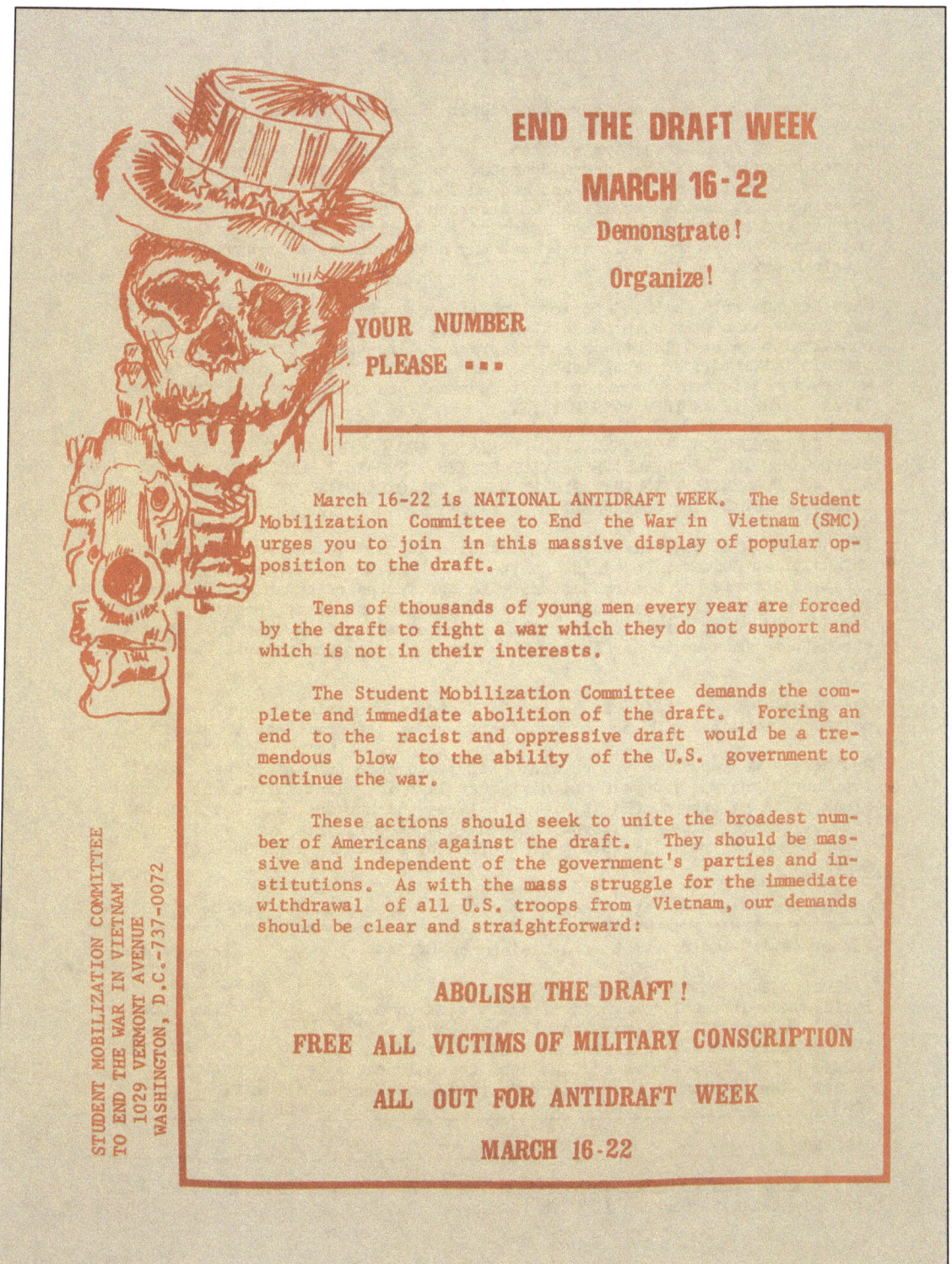

The military draft, administered by the Selective Service System, was the process through which the federal government secured soldiers to fight in Vietnam. The draft was basically involuntary military service with serious penalties for non-compliance. National Antidraft Week was held in 1970, evidence that the draft continued to be a major target of anti-war protest activities for several years.

```
                         T H E  R E S I S T A N C E

A message to our young brothers and sisters from the Resistance:

We, as young Americans, have watched this country degenerate under the mis-
guided hands of men like Lyndon Johnson.  We have seen this corruption
destroy human life in Vietnam and around the world. And then, surely it
comes home...there is rebellion and disorder in the streets...there is
poverty and privation here.  We look and see a system behind it all.  We
understand that things will never get any better unless that system of
American existance is destroyed.

What has our role in the deterioration of our society been?  That connection
is clearer than ever when the system calls you to be its mercenary.  The
penalty for refusal is prison and disgrace we are told.  How easily we have
been intimidated...how sheepishly we surrender our freedom..how grateful
we are for deferments from the draft..."thank you master" echoes from our
lips.  THERE IS ANOTHER POSSIBILITY.

     ON OCTOBER 16, 1967, WE WILL PUBLICILY AND COLLECTIVELY  RETURN OUR
DRAFT CARDS TO THE SELECTIVE SERVICE SYSTEM. FROM THAT MOMENT ON, WE
WILL NOT COO. ERATE WITH THAT SYSTEM UNDER ANY CIRCUMSTANCES, REGARDLESS
OF ANY THREAT BY THE GOVERNMENT.

This action will take place in major cities across the country...New York,
Phiadelphia, Chicago, Portland, Auston, San Francisco, and more.  It is the
first in a series of confrontations with the forces of human destruction and de-
gradation that rule this country.  If we are serious about creating a decent
world and freeing ourselves from the terror of the old one, we must find the
strength to face up to our fears.  The system is not omnipotent...it is made
up of men.

What have we been afraid of?  Prison?  Losing a promising career?  Being
called a communist?  Or is it just facing up to the truth about ourselves?

Brothers— we appeal to you to stop hiding and come out and fight.  Fight
for the future you and your childern must live in.  That future will remain
bleak until we try to mold it with our lives and our dreams.  You are not
free...you are being used...you arebeing bought off.  How long will you
tolerate having your life being controlled by something like Selective
Service?

Around the world  men are fighting the oppressor.  Shall we not be with them.
====================================================================================
Please detach and return to the Resistance Office       · ---      The Resistance
                                                                    1093 Broxton Ave
I wish to support the Resistance YES_No_                            rm. 238
I will unconditionally turn in my draft card on Oct,16___           L.A. 90024
I will send in my draft card to the Resistance office on           Ph. 473-6410
the condition that it will not be sent to my draft board               879-9440
unless 500 of my brothers in L.A. send in their cards___
Please keep in contact with me for meetings and work in the office___
NAME_____PHONE_____

ADDRESS_____

If you know of a group which wishes to know more of the RESISTANCE, we will
send a speaker to discuss it with them.
```

Members of the Resistance viewed the draft as a tool for perpetuating a system of oppression, domination, and militarism, both domestically and internationally. They believed that the most meaningful and honorable response to the Selective Service System was total non-cooperation, symbolized by burning draft cards or sending them back. To disengage from the draft in such a confrontational but nonviolent manner required a high level of personal commitment. Participating in the Resistance meant a person was making a political and moral statement, boldly and directly rejecting participation in the war machine, whatever the consequences.

join the:

WOMEN'S MARCH

sat. may 7th, 12:30 p.m.

(DAY BEFORE MOTHER'S DAY)

Assemble for a rally at the U.S. Armory at 33rd Street between Lexington and Park Avenues. We will march across 34th Street through Herald Square up to the Port Authority Bus Terminal. We plan to leaflet and discuss with people along the way and with soldiers and their families at the bus terminal.

(CHILDREN WELCOME)

BRING OUR MEN HOME FROM VIETNAM NOW

More than 3,000 American men have already died and our casualties are mounting rapidly in a war that the American people don't want and the Vietnamese people don't want. The desire of the American people to end this war has been expressed in the press, in the many demonstrations across the country, in the hearings in Washington, and in all the polls taken, as well as in many other ways.

The recent demonstrations in the cities of south Vietnam show that the people there want the war to end too.

American women must speak out to demand that our sons, husbands, brothers, and sweethearts be brought home now.

Although this 1966 march was organized by and for women, it was not focused on women's liberation. Rather, it was advertised as a peaceful protest event in New York City and an attempt to communicate with the public about ending American intervention in Vietnam and bringing our troops home. Even so, the demonstration was an indication of an emerging consciousness among some women that they could and should engage in anti-war actions as a distinct group rather than being absorbed within male-dominated organizations.

Since 1889, the first day of May—International Workers Day—has been a worldwide celebration of the working class, often featuring demonstrations in support of workers' demands to improve their economic status. On May Day, 1967, that cause was linked with opposition to America's involvement in the Vietnam War and to redirecting the funds spent for war to meet domestic needs by providing affordable basic services to people. Throughout the course of the war, May Day continued to be a date when large protests for both causes occurred. New York City was the location for this particular rally.

WE, PEOPLE FROM ALL WALKS OF LIFE, DECLARE AN END TO OUR SILENCE. WE DECLARE IT PARTICULARLY TO THE GOVERNMENT OF THE UNITED STATES.

MEN CRIED FOR JUSTICE
YOU MOCKED THEM WITH THE LAW OF GUNS

MEN HUNGERED
YOU LAID WASTE THEIR FIELDS

MEN SOUGHT BROTHERHOOD
YOU ANSWERED WITH WAR AGAINST A COLORED PEOPLE

MEN SEARCHED FOR FREEDOM
YOU IMPOSED PUPPETS AND TYRANTS UPON THEM

MEN TRIED TO BUILD
YOU BURNED THEM WITH NAPALM

MEN VOTED FOR PEACE
YOU ESCALATED WAR

In Vietnam you create a wasteland and kill indiscriminately and call it "pacification."

At home you betray the dispossessed, conscript the youth of the nation for war, and call it "democracy."

WE CALL ALL AMERICANS to unite and mobilize in a movement to end the senseless slaughter of American GI's and the mass murder of Vietnamese.

We call for the enlistment of the men, money and resources now being used to maintain the military machine in a fight against the real enemies

of man —

hunger, hopelessness, ignorance, hate, fear, discrimination and inequality.

to the mothers and fathers whose sons are taken

to the gi's who face death

to the youth filled with the love of life, drafted to take the lives of others

to the black people and other minorities who are tired of fighting for a "democracy" they have never enjoyed

to labor, facing higher taxes and prices while war profits soar and pressures are applied against wage increases and the right to strike

to the farmers caught in the "cost-price" squeeze and being taxed off their land

to professionals, businessmen and others who are disturbed about the war and are anxious to see it end

to the clergy who call all men to be brothers and who are mocked by this slaughter

The location, year, and source of this leaflet are not known, but the message was aimed at a variety of audiences, particularly the U.S. government: Stop the killing of Americans and Vietnamese and instead devote resources to addressing social, economic, cultural, environmental, and educational problems at home and abroad.

Join the American Servicemen's Union

"To win a Bill of Rights for rank and file servicemen and women"

WE DEMAND:

1. The right to refuse to obey illegal orders -- like orders to fight in the illegal, imperialist war in Southeast Asia.

2. Election of officers by vote of the rank and file.

3. An end to saluting and sir-ing of officers.

4. The right of Black, Latin and other national minority servicemen and women to determine their own lives free from the oppression of racist whites. No troops to be sent into Black, Latin or other national minority communities.

5. No troops to be used against anti-war demonstrators.

6. No troops to be used against workers on strike.

7. Rank and file control of court-martial boards.

8. The right of free political association.

9. Federal minimum wages.

10. The right of collective bargaining.

**READ THE BOND,
ASU NEWSPAPER**

MILITARY INJUSTICE

To Andy Stapp, Chairman, American Servicemen's Union, Room 737, 150 Fifth Avenue, New York, New York 10011

I am a rank-and-file enlisted man or woman.
I hereby declare that I support the American Servicemen's Union and enclose two dollars to register myself as a member. As a Union member I agree to support other union members in our effort to gain our rights. As a member I will receive a copy of The GI's Handbook on Military Injustice and a subscription to The BOND and any other advice and instruction issued by central union organizers. I will also contact the union center for advice in case of emergency and keep the center informed in order to aid other union members.

name and rank --

military address --

base, ship or area (if APO or FPO)--------------------------

military phone (if in US)------------------------------------

home address ---

date getting out --

home phone ---

ASU   Room 737   150 5th Ave., New York, N.Y.10011

In 1966, activist Andy Stapp decided that his efforts toward ending the Vietnam War would be more effective by organizing inside the military. He enlisted in the Army, hoping to persuade his fellow soldiers to speak out against American intervention in Vietnam. To pursue this bold and risky form of anti-war protest, Private Stapp founded the American Servicemen's Union on Christmas Day, 1967. At its peak in the early 1970s, the ASU claimed more than ten thousand members and each month distributed fifteen thousand copies of its newspaper, *The Bond*.

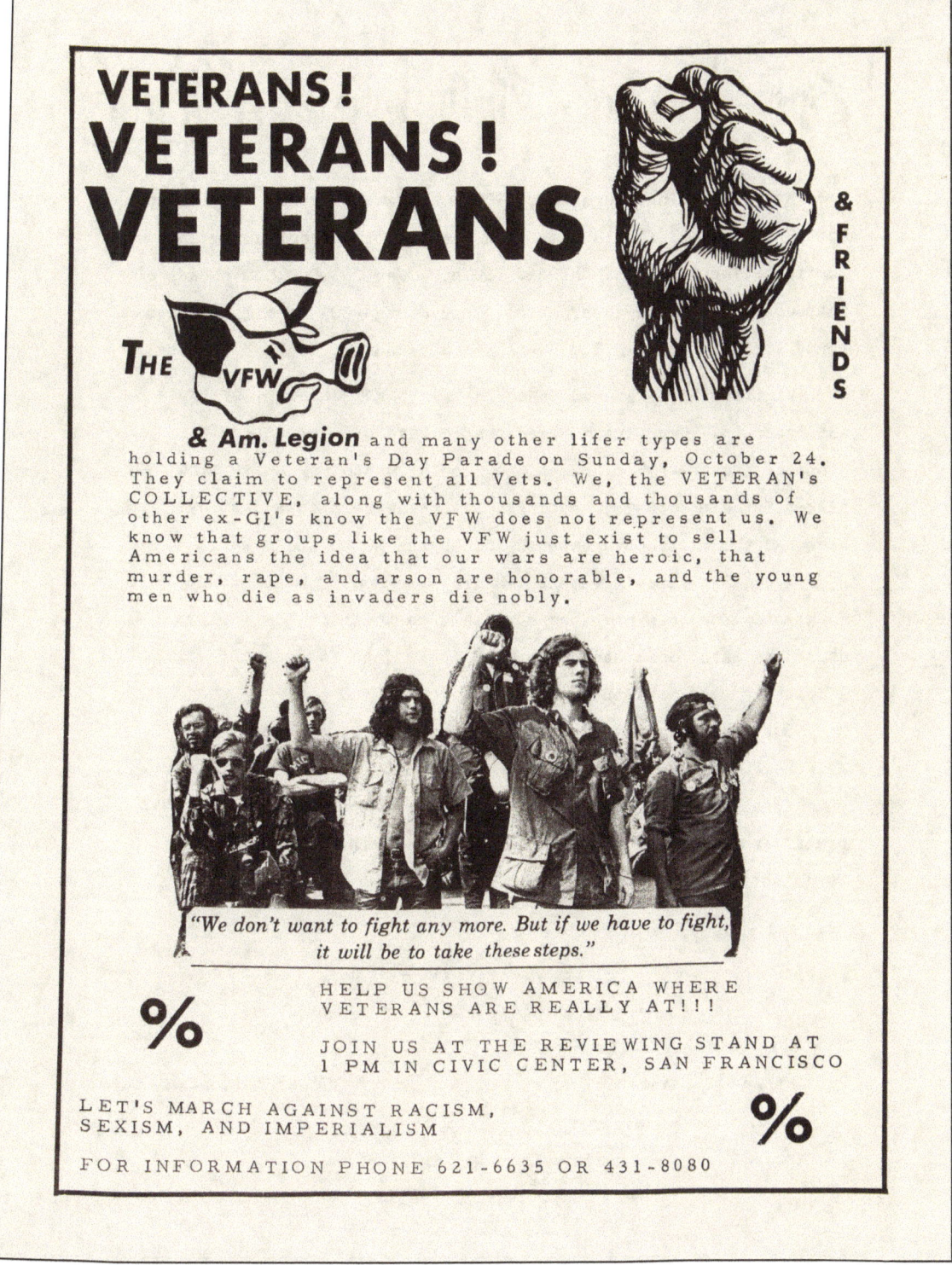

Anti-war statements and actions by those who had fought in Vietnam were particularly powerful because veterans had seen firsthand the horrors of combat. This 1971 leaflet expresses disillusionment with military service, a common response among veterans to their experience in Vietnam. Veterans who strongly rejected the patriotic mythology surrounding the Vietnam War also became acutely aware of other contradictions and inequalities in American society. As the leaflet says, "Let's march against racism, sexism, and imperialism."

Port Chicago Vigil Needs You!

Every day since August 6, 1966, the Naval Weapons Station at Port Chicago, California, has been the site of a continuing anti-war confrontation--the PORT CHICAGO VIGIL. Over 200,000,000 pounds of weapons pass through these gates every month--80% of all munitions bound for Vietnam--T.N.T., Napalm, and recently, Nuclear Weapons.

Vigilers have watched Death roll in night and day, by truck and by train. Over one hundred people have been arrested for stopping trucks--for blocking the flow of Death for a few minutes. Picketers have suffered beatings, have had their cars destroyed, have had their lives threatened for saying NO to LBJ's war.

A dynamic peace movement has grown in Contra Costa County. Workers on the base have begun to talk to their fellow workers about the war. Some have even quit their jobs to join the Vigil. A dent has been made in the war.

But dents are not enough. <u>The war must be stopped now!</u> We, the PORT CHICAGO VIGIL, need your help. We need your bodies, your ideas, and your money. We welcome everyone who opposes this brutal and senseless war. We are the last line of domestic resistance.

We need you....

Daily Picket 9AM - 5PM

Waterfront Rd. Gate, Port Chicago

For information and rides call:

339-9668 (East Bay)   or   376-4621 (Contra Costa)

or write:

Port Chicago Vigil
Box 310
Canyon, Calif. 94516

Other forms of opposition to the War in Vietnam were nonviolent and confrontational protests at specific installations that were vital to producing, supplying, or transporting weapons. One such site was the Naval Weapons Station at Port Chicago in California's Contra Costa County. The tone of this announcement about the regular vigil and picket, and the occasional blockade of munitions trucks, is intense and urgent, reflecting the dedication and commitment of those who chose Port Chicago as the place to make their anti-war statement.

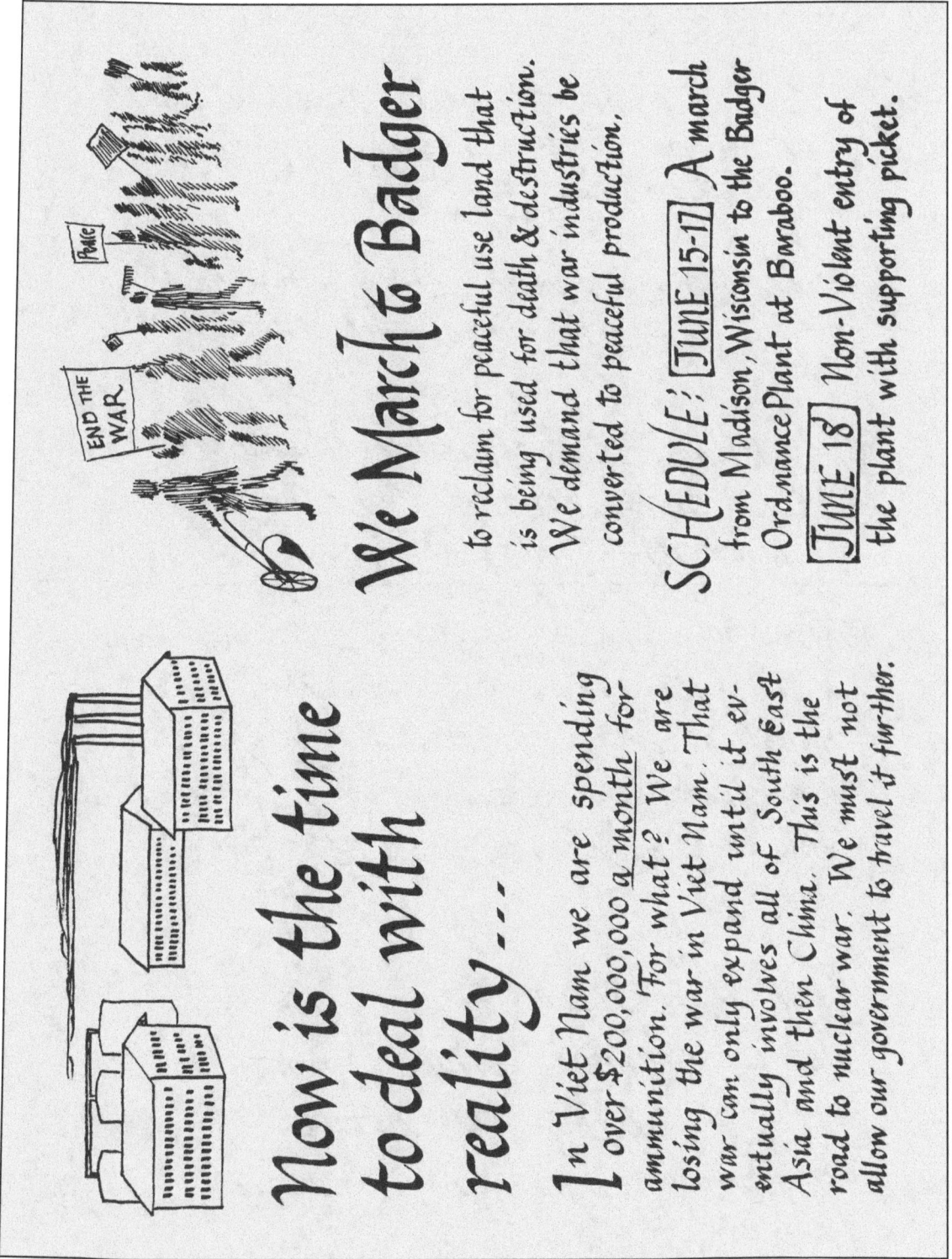

The Badger Ordnance Plant at Baraboo, Wisconsin, was the destination for an anti-war protest march that called for conversion of the facility from "being used for death and destruction . . . to peaceful production." As another Badger leaflet stated, this was a choice between the "Arms Race or the Human Race."

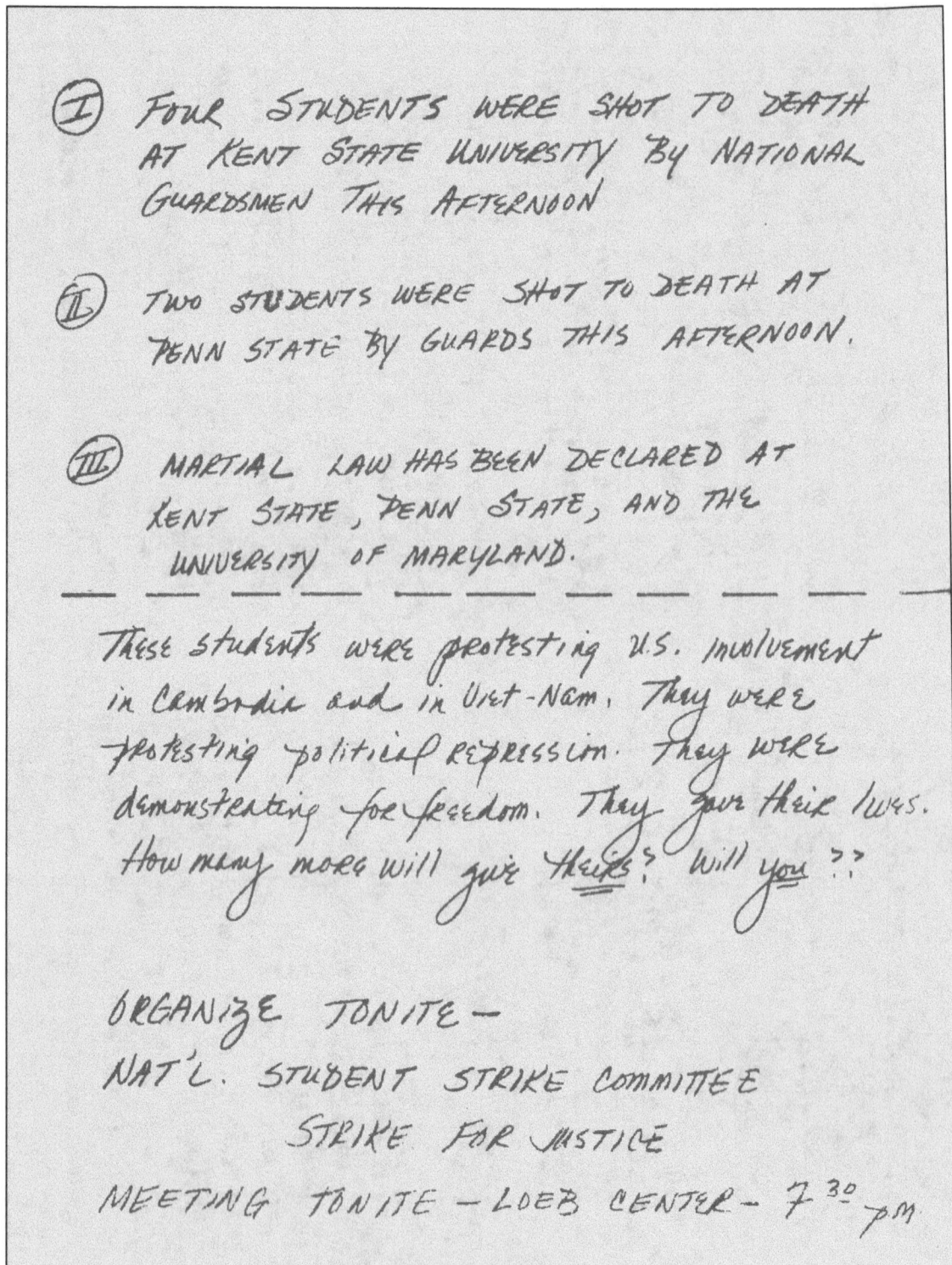

Ⓘ FOUR STUDENTS WERE SHOT TO DEATH AT KENT STATE UNIVERSITY BY NATIONAL GUARDSMEN THIS AFTERNOON

Ⓘ TWO STUDENTS WERE SHOT TO DEATH AT PENN STATE BY GUARDS THIS AFTERNOON.

Ⓘ MARTIAL LAW HAS BEEN DECLARED AT KENT STATE, PENN STATE, AND THE UNIVERSITY OF MARYLAND.

These students were protesting U.S. involvement in Cambodia and in Viet-Nam. They were protesting political repression. They were demonstrating for freedom. They gave their lives. How many more will give theirs? Will you??

ORGANIZE TONITE —
NAT'L. STUDENT STRIKE COMMITTEE
STRIKE FOR JUSTICE
MEETING TONITE — LOEB CENTER — 7³⁰ PM

Four students at Kent State University were shot dead by members of the Ohio National Guard on May 4, 1970, the day this leaflet was written by students at Amherst College in Massachusetts. There had been nationwide demonstrations, including at Kent State, against the Nixon Administration's military expansion into Cambodia, which was an attempt to stop the flow of North Vietnamese soldiers entering South Vietnam. Following the Kent State shootings, massive student strikes involving colleges, universities, and high schools were organized across the country.

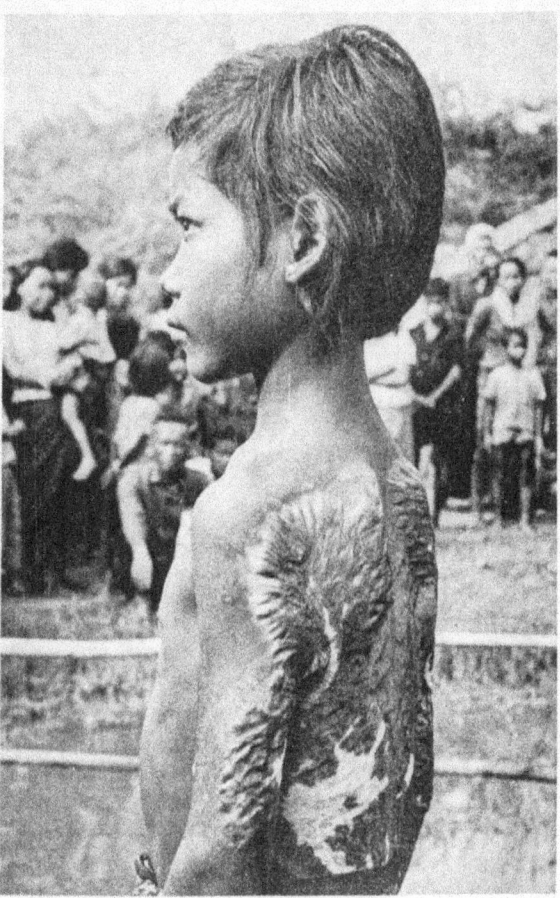

WE ARE BURNING CHILDREN IN VIETNAM

OUR NAPALM DID THIS

NAPALM --- a napalm bomb burst sprays out flaming gasoline jelly. It sticks to the skin.

WRITE - ASK PRESIDENT JOHNSON TO STOP NAPALM BOMBING

DISTRIBUTE THIS FLYER IN YOUR COMMUNITY $8.50 per 1000
(Specify whether you want your name at the bottom)

TED MOYNAHAN 54 SPRING STREET NEW YORK, N.Y.

Many leaflets were created to promote events, while others were designed to draw attention to specific issues or particularly horrifying aspects of the Vietnam War such as the use of napalm bombs. In those pre-internet days, a master layout could be supplied to individuals or groups who would then add contact information at the bottom for leaflets to be reproduced and distributed in their local communities.

SECTION 3

Ethnic Identity and Solidarity

DURING THE SIXTIES, separate but related efforts for political power, economic advancement, and cultural expression pursued by Puerto Rican Americans, Hispanic and Latino
Americans, Asian Americans, and Native Americans paralleled similar activities by African Americans.

The United Farm Workers, based in Delano, California, organized a lengthy strike
against growers of table grapes to establish collective-bargaining rights for predominantly
Hispanic and Latino field workers. The UFW was fighting for better wages, improved working conditions, and higher living standards, and it encouraged the boycott of grocery stores
that sold grapes from growers who refused to negotiate. Some Asian Americans viewed the
Vietnam War as an example of racist imperialism by the United States, in which the Vietnamese were struggling for national self-determination and against the colonial exploitation of a foreign power. The American Indian Movement fought against the subordination
of Native Americans by insisting on cultural dignity for tribal communities and greater
political independence from federal government agencies. The Young Lords were active in
urban Puerto Rican "barrios," monitoring police behavior and delivering a range of social,
health, and educational programs and services very much like the Black Panther Party for
Self-Defense did in Black neighborhoods.

Different ethnic groups pursued various pathways in defining their distinctive cultural
identities. As those processes evolved, however, there was the simultaneous realization that
they had been collectively marginalized and victimized by the prevailing White political
and economic structure. These common, shared experiences led to themes of solidarity:
"Fight All National Oppression" said one leaflet; "Unity for Survival" stated another; "Rally
Against Racism, War, Repression" announced a third. A leaflet from the Young Patriots and
Young Lords proclaimed these slogans: "Destroy the Establishment"; "Free Oppressed
People"; "All Power to the People!"

THE ASIAN DECLARATION TO AMERICA

As Asian People in America, we condemn the United States government for its
massive acts of atrocity in Southeast Asia and in Asian communities at home. We
mourn the deaths of over one million Vietnamese, countless Laotians and Cambodians,
as well as deaths of Asians in our communities from tuberculosis, malnutrition, and
suicide. We are outraged by the wanton destruction of cities, villages, and
countryside in Asia, and by the destruction of our communities at home For too
long our people have been the victims of a cruel and insensitive Western domination,
and have not been able to fully live a life of self-determination. We believe that
Asian People have the right to life, liberty, and the pursuit of happiness. The
United States government is guilty of policies which take away those rights This
must end Now. Therefore, we demand of the United States government:

    1. The immediate end to the Asian War via,

        a. the withdrawal of all American military bases, personnel, and

          weaponry from Asia.

        b. an end to American political interference via the Central

          Intelligence Agency, Agency for International Development (AID),

          and other forms of so called "foreign aid"

    2. An end to American Exploitation by big business of raw materials, land,

       and labor of Asian People and other Third World People at home and abroad.

    3. The recognition of the right of self-determination by Asian, Native

       American, Black, Brown, and other oppressed communities to transform

       War resources into tools for rebuilding communities at home.

On strike: Get To Work

We are striking not to shut down the University, but to redirect the energy of
every person and to use the University personnel to actively work against the War
Machine. More importantly, we must work against all elements in American Society
that make such ugly systems (such as the Asian War) possible and inevitable.
We will educate and mobilize the Asian community on campus to unite with the rest
of our community, to stop the Asian War, and to eliminate all the root problems
that make any unjust war possible.

DARE TO STRUGGLE, DARE TO WIN!!

The leaflet's authors are unknown, other than "Asian People." The location is also unknown, with a reference only to "the University." The declaration contains no visual elements, as if they would detract from the message. And what a powerful, strident, direct message it is: viewing America's Vietnam War, in essence, as an embodiment of racism, linking the brutal treatment of Asian populations in Southeast Asia to the discrimination that they face in the United States, and connecting with other marginalized peoples to demand an end to oppression and the opportunity for self-determination—that is, for life, liberty, and the pursuit of happiness.

Join the NON-VIOLENT STRIKE for JUSTICE

Walter Reuther (UAW) joins Cesar Chavez and the United Farm Workers in the Delano Grape Strike picket line on December 16, 1965.

5TH YEAR OF STRIKE!
The Grape Strike is now in its fifth year. California and Arizona farm workers continue their strike against table grape growers who refuse to recognize their union and their right to live and work with dignity. The farm workers ask only the same rights and benefits which most American workers have enjoyed for decades.

FARM WORKERS NEED YOUR HELP
This is the third year of the table grape boycott and the struggle to bring table grape growers to the bargaining table. Most growers still refuse to recognize the farm workers' union and their workers' right to collective bargaining. Farm workers need your support of the grape boycott to bring these growers to the bargaining table. Only when growers and workers sit down together and sign a fair union contract can this dispute be ended. Only when farm workers enjoy the benefits and protections of the contract can they begin to free their lives of social and economic bondage.

DON'T BUY NON-UNION GRAPES

A few growers have recently signed the first table grape contracts with the United Farm Workers. These contracts provide some of the best wages and working conditions that field workers have ever enjoyed. They also afford protection from pesticides to workers and consumers alike.

Buy grapes only if you are sure they came out of a box with this emblem on it.  UNION LABEL

A BELL FOR DELANO — The "Delano Freedom Bell" is now traveling the country in a van provided by UAW to promote the grape boycott. The 300 pound bell, cast by the famous Whitechapel Bell Foundry of London, England, is a gift from friends of the Farm Workers. On April 17, 1970, Cesar Chavez asked mayor John Lindsay and Dean Francis Sayre to silence the bell with chains as a symbol of farm workers' enslavement to poverty and paternalism. The chains will be broken from the bell only when the grape workers of California and Arizona are free to bargain collectively for their wages and working conditions.

If you would like to help the cause or would like more information, contact your local boycott committee or people representing organized labor, or write to: United Farm Workers Organizing Committee AFL-CIO, P. O. Box 130, Delano, California 93215.

In the mid-1960s, the United Farm Workers, under the leadership of Cesar Chavez, began a campaign to pressure growers of table grapes in California and Arizona to enter into contracts raising the wages of agricultural laborers and improving their working and living conditions. The UFW encouraged consumers not to purchase grapes from companies that refused to negotiate. ("UAW" is the United Auto Workers; *Huelga* means "strike" in Spanish; "NFWA" is the National Farm Workers Association; "AWOC" is the Agricultural Workers Organizing Committee; "AFL-CIO" is the American Federation of Labor-Congress of Industrial Organizations, a coalition of unions.)

BOYCOTT SAFEWAY

FARM WORKERS REAP GRAPES OF WRATH

Farm workers still work in 1969 with poor wages, no overtime pay, no health care, poorly reported social security, and no unemployment insurance.

In protest the United Farm Workers Organizing Committee has called an international boycott of all table grapes. This boycott will continue until the grape growers agree to bargain with the farm workers on improvement of conditions.

SAFEWAY STOCKS GRAPES

With 2,172 stores Safeway is the second largest chain store in the nation. In 1967 they sold 3.36 billion dollars worth of goods; they buy about 3 million dollars a year worth of grapes, highest in the nation. Unlike other chain stores and independents they have refused to remove grapes from their shelves.

Unionists and citizens can demand Safeway join other chain stores and independents in removing table grapes from the shelves, thus taking a much needed stand for justice in the fields of California

SIGN THE SAFEWAY PLEDGE

"Therefore, we the undersigned will not shop at Safeway stores until Safeway makes a public announcement they will not handle California table grapes for the duration of the boycott."

For information on Safeway Boycott Petitions contact:
Citizen's Don't Buy Grapes Committee
263 Andover St.
San Francisco 94110

The campaign to boycott Safeway was part of the effort by the United Farm Workers to persuade growers of table grapes to provide farm workers with decent wages, improved working and living conditions, and benefits. ("Grapes of Wrath" refers to a novel by John Steinbeck published in 1939 and set in the Great Depression of the 1930s; the novel depicts the struggles of a family of tenant farmers forced by adverse economic and environmental circumstances to leave Oklahoma in search of a better life in California.)

DEMONSTRATION

FOR WOUNDED KNEE
UNITED PEOPLE
AIM

IN SUPPORT OF THE PAN-AMERICAN QUEST FOR JUSTICE, THE AMERICAN INDIAN MOVEMENT, AND THE DEMANDS OF

THE TRAIL OF BROKEN TREATIES

WEDNESDAY   MARCH 21

FEDERAL BUILDING 12 pm

450 GOLDEN GATE
SAN FRANCISCO, CALIFORNIA

UNITY FOR SURVIVAL

Rides leaving from:
   Berkeley- 11:00am- Dana & Bancroft
   Oakland- 11:00am- 14th & High
   Palo Alto-Redwood City- 11:15 am- People's Medical Center- 2555 Middlefield
   San Jose- 10:30am- 90 S. 2nd. - Indian Center

In late February, 1973, members of the American Indian Movement, led by Dennis Banks and Russell Means, occupied Wounded Knee, on the Pine Ridge Indian Reservation in South Dakota. AIM representatives declared the existence of an independent Oglala Sioux Nation, made demands for local governance, and issued broader complaints about the treatment of Native American tribal lands and communities by the U.S. government. This 1973 demonstration was in support of the Wounded Knee occupation, which symbolized the efforts of Native American tribes across the country to reclaim their ancestral lands and pursue self-determination.

Who are Los Siete ?

Seven brothers framed by the fascist power structure of San Francisco--
seven brothers set up because of their participation in the Brown Liberation
Movement. These Siete: Tony and Mario Martinez, Nelson Rodriguez, Jose
Rios, Danilo Melendez, Gary Lescallett and George Lopez--worked for all
Brown people, for all the people, for self determination. These Siete
worked recruiting brothers and sisters to go to college, in making their
people aware of the injustices of a society in which we are taught to
fight our brothers.

Los Siete are now on trial for their lives, facing charges of murder and
attempted murder, for the death of Joseph Brodnik, a pig famous for his
treatment of young people in the Mission District. The circumstances
are unclear--what is clear is the persecution of brothers who worked in the
community to better it.

Los Siete stand for all the opression of all poor, working class people
Theyare a symbol, a rallying point in Brown Liberation because they stand
 for every Brown brother harrassed on every street in this country. They
symbolize the youth working for change, trying to make a better country
in which to live. They are our brothers. And this is not isolated--any
one of our people could have been a Los Siete. Any one who stands up
against the system, for the people, could have been the victim of this
fascist oppression. Los Siete are special because they choose to fight
back, not to bow down to the system.

What is Los Siete ?

Los Siete is an organization dedicated to serving the people. Los Siete
has set up community programs, in which the people have a say-so in their
lives. There is a Los Siete Free Breakfast for School Children, to help
our children working for an education. Breakfast is served every morning
(7-8:30) at 1249 Alabama and 120 Julian. There is a people's restaurant--
EL BASTA YA--which has just opened at 260 Valencia. It needs workers
interested in working for the people. There is a people's news service--
the Basta Ya--which comes out once a month. There are community health
projects to help the people have the medical care they need.

This is Los Siete--a defense organization for the people--so that we can
be free to determine our own destinies.

Free Los Siete with donations--of time, talent, and money. Free Los Siete
with spirit--the will to win. Free Los Siete and bring them back to their
people.

¡Free Los Sietel ⇒RALLY⇐ Nov. 21-12:30 pm Civic Center Plaza, S.F.

For more information: call 621-9166.

"Los Siete" refers to seven Hispanic men involved in the "Brown Liberation Movement" who were charged with serious crimes having to do with the death of a San Francisco policeman. Los Siete was also an organization that offered services to disadvantaged people similar to the programs of the Black Panther Party. The language in the leaflet is strong and militant, with phrases like "the fascist power structure," "a pig" (policeman), "the persecution of brothers," "the system," and "fascist oppression."

This announcement was for the 1968 May Day march and rally in Oakland, California, which honored the achievements of the working class. Addressed specifically to Asian Americans, it calls upon them to join with others to "fight all national oppression." The phrase *Viva la Huelga* translates roughly to "Long Live the Strike," a reference to the activities by the United Farm Workers in California and Arizona to gain union recognition for field workers from growers of table grapes.

MOVE with the LORDS
RALLY! ACTION! DO IT!
11:30 AM TODAY COLUMBIA U.
(116 ST. + BROADWAY)

For over a week the Young Lords organization has occupied the First Spanish Methodist Church (111th and Lexington). They were forced to move into the building because the church would not respond to their many requests for space. The Lords seek to use the resources of the church for the good of El Barrio. They want space for:

1) Free Breakfasts for Children - The system kills in many ways. Hunger and malnutrition must be ended in El Barrio.

2) Liberation Schools - Break through the public school brain-washing. The Lords seek to teach the true history and conditions of Puerto Rico to their people.

3) Day Care Centers - Cooperative day care centers are essential to the liberation of women and to teach children healthy cooperation. The future belongs to the young.

4) Medical Services - The Lords are giving the lead poisoning tests and the iron deficiency tests which the city promised but never delivered.

The young Lords efforts to serve the people must succeed, and we must work to see that happen. Many people have gone to the church and seen the spirit and activity of the people there. But we must understand that although the church building is in El Barrio, the power of the church is with the predominantly white, wealthy hierarchy far from East Harlem. The Methodist Church owns $5 billion in real estate in this country and spends over $100 million for church buildings each year. Those resources have not been used to help people solve their problems but to help make them content and controllable. We must work with the Lords in forcing the Methodist hierarchy to FREE THE SPACE!

11:30 AM   TODAY   COLUMBIA UNIVERSITY   (116th and Broadway)
11:30 AM   TODAY   COLUMBIA UNIVERSITY   (116th and Broadway)

ALL POWER TO THE PEOPLE!

The Young Lords were present in predominantly Puerto Rican urban neighborhoods—"El Barrio"— such as Manhattan's East Harlem in New York City, the location of the First Spanish Methodist Church (111th Street and Lexington Avenue). The demonstration site is Columbia University, on the Upper West Side of Manhattan. The Young Lords provided a variety of social services and responded to incidents of police brutality and misconduct against community residents. The controversy and rally described here concerns the Young Lords requesting space in the church for their activities.

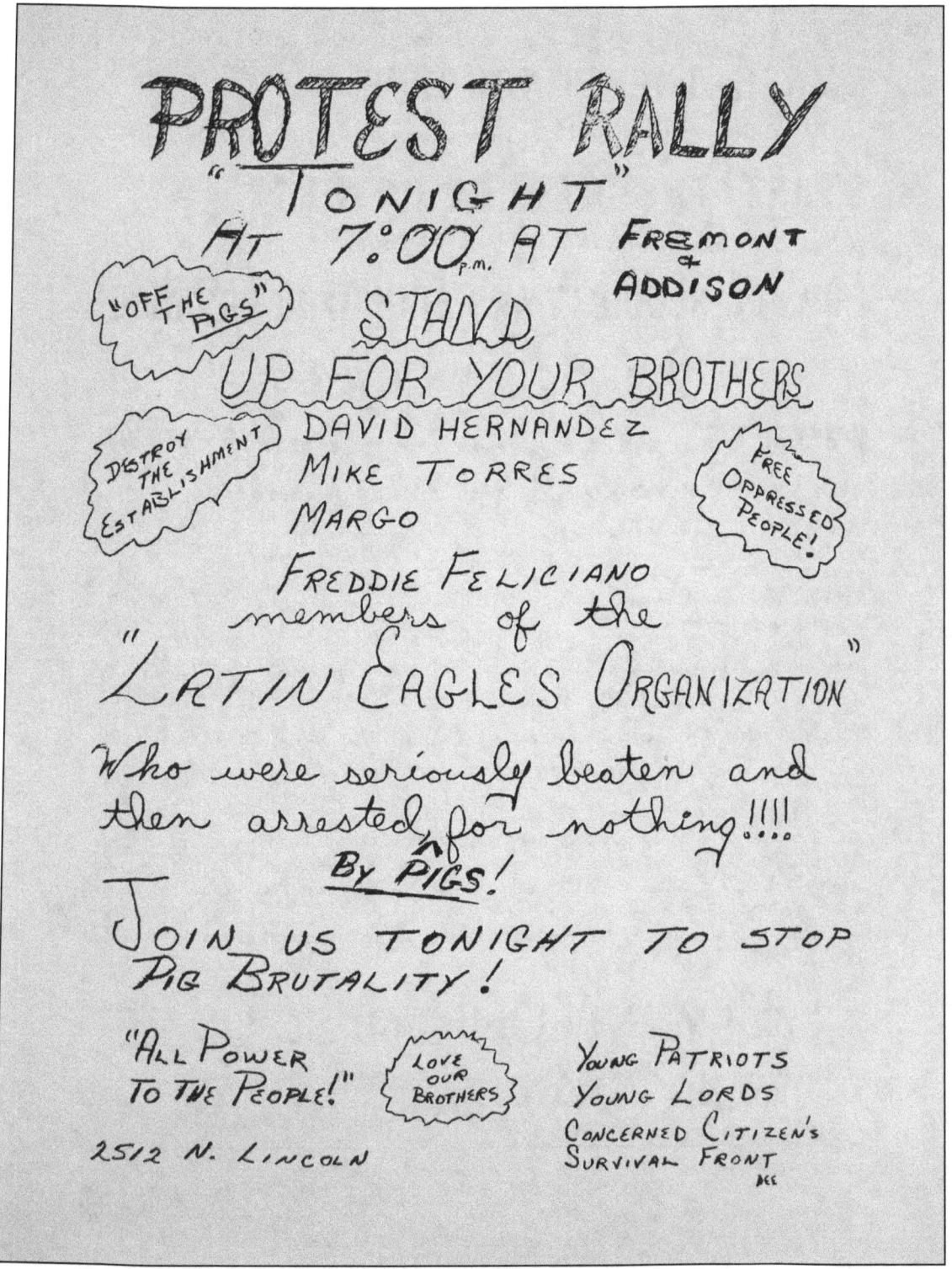

The handwritten informality of this leaflet is one of its notable features, as are the several chants and slogans circled in the text that are representative of radical political language in the Sixties. "Pig" or "pigs" is derogatory slang for the police or other law-enforcement authorities. The phrase "Off the pigs" meant to harm or even kill police officers. The Young Patriots and Young Lords were activist organizations oriented to Puerto Rican, Hispanic, and Latino communities, which offered social services and monitored police activity, much as the Black Panthers did in African American neighborhoods.

SMASH THE FILIBUSTER —

First Class Citizenship for Negroes and Puerto Ricans!

START THE WAR ON POVERTY —

Stop the War in Vietnam!

FOR JOB SECURITY AND ECONOMIC ADVANCE!

Demonstrate

FRIDAY, MAY 1st — 4 to 7 P. M.

UNION SQUARE · 17th St. and Broadway

- 30-Hour Week
- $1.50 Minimum Wage
- Guaranteed Annual Income
- Government Responsibility to Create Jobs
- Create Jobs Through Disarmament and Conversion to Peacetime Economy

- Pass the Civil Rights Bill
- Job Equality for Negro and Puerto Rican Workers
- Integrated-Quality Education
- Full and Equal Citizenship for the Negro and Puerto Rican People

Start the War on Poverty and Stop the War in Vietnam by Withdrawing American Troops

Join in Labor's traditional holiday, born in the fight for the 8-hour day in Chicago in 1886.

Labor has come a long way since then. But Labor's job is still unfinished. Come to Union Square on May Day and demonstrate for peace and peaceful co-existence, jobs and economic security, full social, political and economic equality for the Negro and Puerto Rican people, and a strengthening of our democratic rights.

Join your fellow workers throughout the United States and the world in demonstrating for PEACE, FREEDOM AND JOBS!

RALLY AT UNION SQUARE
MAY DAY 4 – 7 P. M.

Sponsored by: Greater New York Labor Press Club—Room 1033
41 Union Sq. West, New York, N. Y. 10003 · *Phone YU 9-6510*

May Day, the first day of May, is traditionally celebrated in many countries to recognize the contributions of working people; it serves as an occasion to publicize programs and policies that would raise their wages and improve their terms of employment and economic status. This 1964 May Day demonstration in Manhattan presents a broad agenda linking legal, political, economic, and social demands. Particularly striking this early in the Vietnam War was the emphasis on ending U.S. involvement and redirecting resources to improve the living conditions of disadvantaged Americans: "Start the war on poverty and stop the war in Vietnam"; and "Peace, freedom, and jobs!"

**RALLY AGAINST
RACISM, WAR, REPRESSION**
SAN JOSE, SATURDAY MAY 20
1 PM WILLIAM ST. PARK
(SO. 16th & E. WILLIAM)

initial sponsors:

WOMENS INTERNATIONAL LEAGUE FOR PEACE & FREEDOM   PEOPLES COALITION FOR PEACE & JUSTICE
COMMUNITY ALERT PATROL   NATIONAL UNITED COMMITTEE TO FREE ANGELA DAVIS
ASIANS FOR COMMUNITY ACTION   YOUNG WORKERS LIBERATION LEAGUE
SAN JOSE PEACE CENTER   VIETNAM VETERANS AGAINST THE WAR
NATIONAL COMMITTEE AGAINST REPRESSIVE LEGISLATION

This 1972 leaflet appears to portray Angela Davis, an articulate—and at that time imprisoned—proponent of Black Power, embracing various causes and people. Her face is seen again in the upper left, above the symbol for the United Farm Workers, an organization dedicated to unionizing migrant farm laborers. Also included are a Vietnamese woman aiming a rifle toward an American aircraft, and a bearded protester next to an anti-war placard. "*Viva La Raza*" has multiple meanings: "Long live the race," "the race lives," and "long live the people," among others. The phrase is used by Mexican Americans or "Chicanos" to express ethnic awareness and cultural pride.

SECTION 4

Women's Liberation

WOMEN ARE GETTING FED UP! We are getting together to take control of our lives. Women's Liberation is fighting for equal wages, child care, birth control and jobs. We are fighting against oppression on the job, in the home, and in the society. We are fighting for our recognition as equal human beings and for a society that is run in the interests of people not profits.

—Leaflet for International Women's Day, 1970

AS THE CIVIL RIGHTS, Black Power, and anti-war movements gathered momentum between 1963 and 1968, each of them contained internal contradictions that were striking and ironic. Inside the interminable meetings, discussions, planning sessions, strategic and tactical debates, and social gatherings, women starting looking around at supposedly open-minded men, and then at each other. On an intensely personal level, they experienced frustration, anger, and ultimately rage at the demeaning ways with which these men often treated them. They resented being perceived as incapable of serious thinking, as solely makers and deliverers of coffee and providers of physical pleasure. In the conventional world of work and domesticity, such sexism was routine and prevalent. But coming from men committed to freedom for African Americans and to self-determination for Vietnam, this attitude reflected blatant hypocrisy and a stunning lack of self-awareness.

Revolting against this chauvinism and disrespect, female activists focused on issues that immediately impacted them and often organized activities specifically not involving men. Historically, one of the most glaring forms of male supremacy was denying or severely limiting access to abortion. The question was asked time and again across the country: "Why do men who manage the political process at all levels get to decide whether and when women can have children?" The inability to make choices about reproduction and pregnancy directly limited women's opportunities for employment and a career, so they wondered if that negative power was intentional, a way of keeping women down and "in their place."

In response, a 1968 leaflet boldly proclaimed "Abortion is a right!" Some believed that abortion could be a unifying issue, one that might bring women together regardless of ethnicity, religion, socio-economic status, occupation, or sexual orientation. Another leaflet spoke broadly about the lack of control "over our bodies . . . and . . . our reproductive lives" and expressed strident outrage: "No more fear of demanding those rights which are ours!"

A national campaign to establish federal protection for abortion culminated in the January 22, 1973, Supreme Court case *Roe v. Wade*, which recognized a constitutional right to abortion. The matter was never really settled politically and culturally, however, and there ensued decades of passionate debate about the moral and medical implications of abortion. For some, the anti-abortion cause became an obsession of singular importance, rising above everything else. Nearly fifty years after *Roe*, on June 24, 2022, a majority conservative Supreme Court rejected this precedent and effectively turned the future of abortion and reproductive rights over to states with the decision in *Dobbs v. Jackson Women's Health Organization*. And states with Republican governors and legislatures were ready, moving almost immediately to severely restrict and even effectively ban the availability of abortion services.

Several leaflets in this section exemplify the ways that women opposed to the Vietnam War asserted themselves by conducting demonstrations for women only, realizing as they did so an uplifting empowerment. A leaflet promoting an anti-war protest action encouraged women to reject traditional roles as only "wives, mothers, and lovers" and instead "assert the right to redefine who we are, as people." Another leaflet, proclaiming, "End the war! End our oppression!" connected the continuation of America's military intervention in Vietnam with the denial of advancement and emancipation to women at home:

> This war is but one manifestation of a system that oppresses people everywhere on many levels. . . . As long as resources are squandered on war, the demands of women's liberation for free abortion; free 24-hour child care; equal pay, employment, and education will not be met.

More fundamentally, stating the primal fact that they are the source of life, women claimed a special role to fulfill in opposing the Vietnam War—not only for policy or ideological reasons but more basically for humanitarian ones.

The movement for women's liberation accelerated with women-only "consciousness raising" groups and celebrations of the special qualities of feminism. One leaflet invited women to "Dance with sisters . . . and rap, eat, listen to music, groove." Another found a common theme of male domination among the manner in which men degraded and objectified women, racism toward non-White minorities, and widespread environmental pollution. The leaflet reached this broad conclusion:

The liberation of woman from the submissive and inferior position in society is essential in changing the relationship of man to the environment . . . and in creating a society that can live in harmony with the environment and not destroy it.

Indeed, the degrading and demeaning treatment of women revealed to some a linkage with the destructive consequences of men exercising their power and privilege:

They have raped the land and women. . . . They have created a dangerous world of nuclear weapons, death-trap highways, inhuman prisons, endless wars, and poisonous air, land, and water.

There was a hopeful belief that a resurgent feminism would make the workplace more humane and less competitive, lead to a kinder, gentler environmentalism, and reduce materialistic consumption with more of an emphasis on human contact and intimacy.

Realization of their oppression by women was a very personal experience. Yet because it was grounded in an identity formed by gender, this realization had the potential to encompass women of many cultural backgrounds and political persuasions. Since the realization of oppression was deeply personal, it was potent and powerful, leading to sweeping perspectives such as this one:

Radical Women is an organization dedicated to exposing, resisting and eliminating discrimination against women in jobs and professions, education, legal status, social freedoms, political life, and family/sexual roles.

One woman's individual manifesto was a leaflet titled "Liberation Is Fulfillment" but it was directed to a large audience:

What we have discovered is that we all have classic stories of being brutalized, mishandled, kept down, abused, underpaid, over-worked, unappreciated, and slapped around in a variety of ways.

What emerged from the 1960s women's liberation movement was a comprehensive agenda that responded to pervasive institutional and structural inequalities centered on priorities such as abortion rights, the availability of birth control, paid maternity leave, the provision of childcare facilities, equal pay and job opportunities, the end of sexual and occupational stereotyping, and funding for educational and training programs. Decades later, that agenda is still a work in progress, as the fight for women's equality and liberation is carried on by a younger generation.

ABORTION IS
A RIGHT!

Fundamental to the liberation of women is our right as free individuals to exercise control over our own bodies on the basis of our own judgement.

We refuse to be considered "criminals" and forced to resort to degrading and dangerous means when we attempt to control our own lives and prevent the birth of unplanned children that wreck the chances for economic independence and a decent standard of living for ourselves and our families. We bear the children, we bear the responsibility, and we demand and deserve the right to make such decisions.

RADICAL WOMEN

Radical Women is an organization dedicated to exposing, resisting and eliminating discrimination against women in jobs and professions, education, legal status, social freedoms, political life, and family/sexual roles. We believe that the oppression of women in this society is a first-priority political, legal, and economic question, and that its solution will come only with a radical change in the political, legal, and economic structure of society.

For further information contact:
Jill Severn, Chairman
2940 36th Avenue South
Seattle, Washington 98144
PA 5-0471   PA 5-1224

March 28, 1968

Proclaiming that women have an inalienable right to an abortion as a private matter without governmental interference was the starting point for a pervasive, deep critique of their subordinate treatment in America. Such an analysis led to the ambitious mission of Radical Women: "an organization dedicated to exposing, resisting and eliminating discrimination against women in jobs and professions, education, legal status, social freedoms, political life, and family/sexual roles." Given the widespread nature of this discrimination and oppression, "its solution will come only with a radical change in the political, legal, and economic structure of society."

EMERGENCY DEMONSTRATION
IN ALBANY ON
ABORTION

■ FREE ABORTION ON DEMAND
  NO FORCED STERILIZATION

■ REPEAL ALL ABORTION &
  CONTRACEPTION LAWS

Ithaca Women's Liberation
Medical Committee for Human Rights
New England Women's Coalition
Rhode Island Coalition for Repeal
 of Abortion Laws
Rochester Women's Center
International Socialist

Sponsors include *

Bella Abzug, Congresswoman
Lucinda Cisler, NYALR, NOW
Ruth Gage Colby, WILPF
Sarah Doely, Churchwomen United
Florence Fenster, ITU
Betty Friedan, NOW
Lucille Iverson, Radical Feminists
Judge Dorothy Kenyon
Kate Millett, writer
Georgiana Pierce, Queen's YWCA
Doris Sassower, Prof. Women Caucus
Althea Simmons, Nat'l. Bd. NAACP
Gloria Steinem, writer

* organizations listed for identification only

Saturday MARCH 27 1:00PM
Rally at the State Capitol
cnr. State & South Hawk
Albany NY

30 bills are now in N.Y. State legislature to cut back women's
right to abortion -- eg., Abortion only to save a woman's life.
Women must join to fight these attempts to deny us our rights!

- -

WOMEN'S STRIKE COALITION, #405, 118 E. 28 St., N.Y., N.Y. 10016
Phone: (212) 685-4106 for further information.

——Manhattan
Enclosed is $____ for ____# bus tickets. ($7/round-trip ticket). ___Bklyn.
All mail orders must be pre-paid by March 22. Busses leave 8 AM ___Queens
from the following points (please check one).   ——Bronx

___I am driving & have room   ___Enclosed is $____to help build March 27.
   for ____.   ___Add me/my organization to March 27
                                        sponsors list.

21

In 1971, women's rights advocates rallied at the New York State Capitol in Albany to oppose attempts by the legislature to dramatically restrict abortion access. Among the protest sponsors were some of the most articulate spokespersons for women's liberation both then and in the following decades, including Bella Abzug, Betty Friedan, Kate Millett, Althea Simmons, and Gloria Steinem. Unrestricted availability of abortion and contraception services was viewed by many women as a clearly fundamental right that had to be established and protected. Without it, predominantly male politicians held the power to make decisions about women's bodies and their reproductive futures.

ABORTION ACTION WEEK
May 1-6, 1972

Repeal all abortion & contraception laws
No more forced sterilization

MAY 2—FILE CLASS-ACTION SUIT CHALLENGING CALIF. ABORTION LAW

MAY 6—DEMONSTRATION IN SACRAMENTO
ASSEMBLE AT CITY PLAZA (9th & I Sts.)—NOON
RALLY AT CAPITOL STEPS—1:00 PM

DEMONSTRATIONS/RALLIES/DEBATES/FILMS/SPEAKOUTS/TEACH-INS/FORUMS/TV TALK SHOWS
SCHOOL ASSEMBLY PROGRAMS /WOMEN AND THEIR BODIES/DISPLAYS/EDUCATION/
RADIO SHOWS/COURT ACTIONS/PICKET LINES/BUTTON SALES/LETTERS TO THE EDITOR

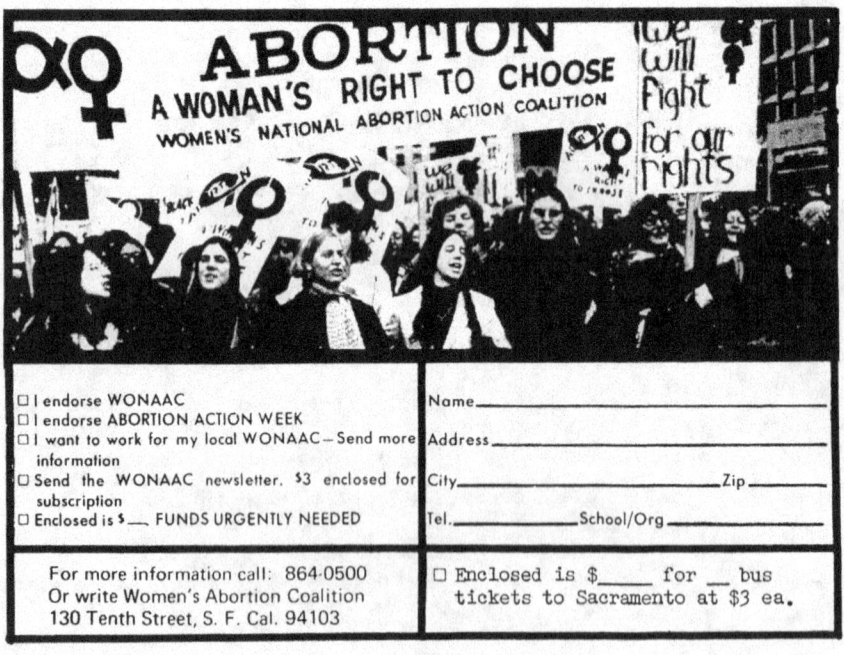

☐ I endorse WONAAC
☐ I endorse ABORTION ACTION WEEK
☐ I want to work for my local WONAAC—Send more information
☐ Send the WONAAC newsletter. $3 enclosed for subscription
☐ Enclosed is $___ FUNDS URGENTLY NEEDED

Name_____
Address_____
City_____Zip_____
Tel._____School/Org_____

For more information call: 864-0500
Or write Women's Abortion Coalition
130 Tenth Street, S. F. Cal. 94103

☐ Enclosed is $____ for __ bus tickets to Sacramento at $3 ea.

The Women's National Abortion Action Coalition organized a series of political, cultural, and media activities in Sacramento, California, to protest state legislative efforts restricting abortion access. "Abortion—a woman's right to choose" was a prevalent theme in the fight for reproductive rights during the late 1960s and early 1970s.

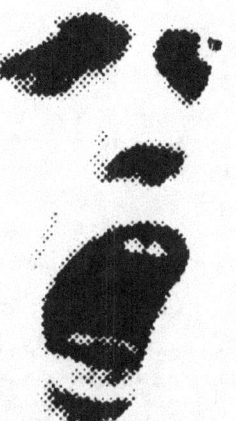

INTERNATIONAL TRIBUNAL ON ABORTION, CONTRACEPTION AND FORCED STERILIZATION

March 9, 10, 11
New York City

On March 9, 10, and 11, 1973, women from all over the United States and from other parts of the world will gather in New York in observance of International Women's Day and for an historic event: the International Tribunal on Abortion, Contraception, and Forced Sterilization. Through the testimony of women from all backgrounds and experiences, and through the testimony of legal and medical experts, we will draw together the evidence necessary to indict the government, the anti-abortion forces, and all those institutions responsible for denying women control over our bodies. We will also hold a demonstration during the Tribunal to present our indictments and our demands directly to those we find guilty of crimes against women.

The Tribunal will hear testimony from Black women, Latina women, Chicanas, Native American and Asian women, gay women, high school and college women, working women, women in the military, and Catholic women. The testimonies will describe the experiences women have been forced to endure because we lack control over our reproductive lives. The Tribunal will hear the sufferings of those who have experienced illegal abortions, who have been victims of forced sterilization, who have been forced to bear children against their will, who have been refused contraceptives, who have been raped and unable to obtain abortions; it will hear about those who have died alone in back-alleys from butcher abortions.

The Tribunal will tell the truth. We will say: No more suffering in silence! No more fear of demanding those rights which are ours! The Tribunal will dispel the myths surrounding abortion, contraception, and forced sterilization and give voice to the millions of women who daily suffer from the laws which legislate our bodies. Our Tribunal will be a contribution to the international abortion rights movement, which is seeking to organize half of humanity in the fight to gain the basic human right to control our bodies.

Days of Denunciation of Crimes Against Women

distributed by: WOMEN'S ABORTION COALITION / 620 Sutter / S.F. 94103 / (415) 771 3403

Clip and return to: COMMITTEE FOR THE INTERNATIONAL TRIBUNAL ON ABORTION, CONTRACEPTION AND FORCED STERILIZATION, 150 Fifth Avenue, Rm. 315, N. Y., N. Y. 10011 (212) 675-9150

☐ I would like more information about the Committee.
☐ I want to help build the International Tribunal.
☐ Enclosed is my donation of $_____ to help the work of the Tribunal.

☐ I would like to become active in WONAAC.
☐ I would like more information on WONAAC's activities.

NAME_____ ADDRESS_____

CITY_____ STATE_____ ZIP_____ PHONE_____

SCHOOL/ORGANIZATION_____

The foundation of the women's liberation movement was rooted in the harassment, discrimination, and oppression that women experience around the world, regardless of their ethnicity, nationality, geographic location, age, socio-economic position, education, occupation, political affiliation, marital status, or sexual orientation. While the focus of the 1973 International Tribunal was abortion, the language of this leaflet speaks forcefully about the commonality of the widespread barriers women face on a global basis.

WOMEN
It Is Insufferable!

MALE DOMINATED COURTS AND LEGISLATURES STILL
DICTATE UNJUST ABORTION LAWS THAT DENY US
CONTROL OVER OUR OWN BODIES

Abagail Adams sent her husband a veiled warning in a letter dated 7 May 1776:

"I cannot say that I think you are very generous to the ladies; for, whilst you are proclaiming peace and goodwill to men, emancipating all nations, you insist upon retaining an absolute power over wives. But you must remember, that arbitrary power is like most other things which are very hard, very liable to be broken; and, not withstanding all your wise laws and maxims, we have it in our power not only to free ourselves, but to subdue our masters, and, without violence, throw both your natural and legal authority at our feet!"

What did she have in mind?

What can we women do? What brilliant scheme
Can we, poor souls, accomplish? we who sit
Trimmed and bedizened in our saffron silks,
Our cambric robes, and little finical shoes?

O ladies! Sisters! If we really mean it,
there's but one way.....
We must abstain - each - from the joys of Love.

LYSISTRATA DAY

to Protest Abortion Laws

March 14, 1970

For further information, contact: NARAL   (212) 265 5125

National Association for Repeal of Abortion Laws
250 W. 57th St.
New York, New York 10019

This leaflet proposes a unique approach to fighting judicial and legislative abortion restrictions. Lysistrata was a female character in a play by Aristophanes, presented in Athens in 411 B.C. Her novel strategy to end fighting between competing Greek city-states entailed persuading women to refrain from sexual relations with men as an inducement for them to engage in peace discussions. Fast-forward to Lysistrata Day, 1970: serious proposal, thoughtful humor, or provocative announcement? Ironic that Lysistrata Day, a protest against "unjust abortion laws that deny us control over our own bodies," seeks to use those very bodies, or the withholding of them, as a political weapon.

In addition to being an organizing issue, ensuring access to abortion was a launching pad for examining a broad range of topics concerning the liberation of women. The 1972 Dance With Sisters shows that such explorations could occur at more informal, relaxed, and entertaining events that were intended for women only. It also implies the powerful notion of an inclusive female sisterhood, transcending secular identities and unifying women in a form of primal pan-feminism.

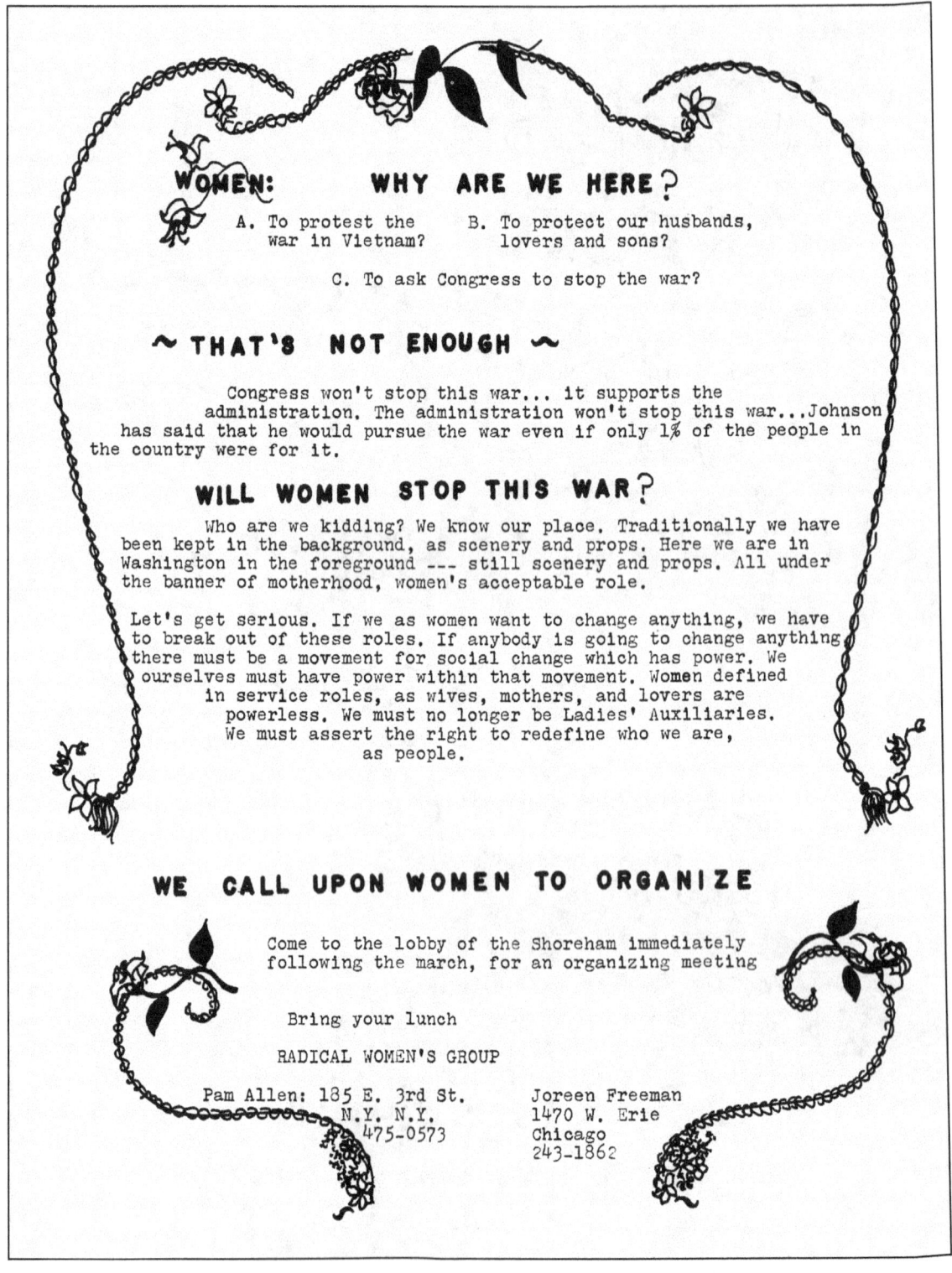

This leaflet expresses the realization by women anti-war activists that, unless traditional gender roles are thoroughly redefined, they will be powerless and subservient to men, even those who proclaim themselves progressive. Influenced by the opposition to America's actions in Vietnam, women came to resist serving as "scenery and props" in male-dominated society, their lives determined under "the banner of motherhood" as "wives, mothers, and lovers." In a radical reaction to such constraints, the leaflet boldly announces, "We must assert the right to redefine who we are, as people," a statement that embodies the emergence of women's consciousness during the late 1960s.

WOMEN: MARCH AGAINST THE WAR

FOR HIM

AND FOR ALL OF AMERICA'S YOUNG MEN

March with us to the Oakland Induction Center where we will present our demands and voice our opposition to the war.

OUR PLANS

On WEDNESDAY, FEBRUARY 23, we will hold an all-woman's march on the Oakland Induction Center.

Women on the Berkeley campus are urged to attend a NOON RALLY on Wednesday. At 1:00 p.m. the march will leave the campus.

Other women who wish to join the march are urged to MEET IT AT 1:15 P.M. AT CONSTITUTION SQUARE IN BERKELEY (Center & Grove).

The march will proceed down Grove & should arrive at the Induction Center at about 3:15 p.m.

Those who will not be able to join the march are urged to MEET AT THE INDUCTION CENTER (14th & Clay) at 3:15 p.m. There will be a rally when the march arrives, and a delegation of women will present the demands of the march to the commander of the induction center, requesting they be conveyed to the President, Commander-in-Chief of the Armed Forces.

We ask that men do not participate in this demonstration. We urge women to dress conservatively, preferably in black.

OUR DEMANDS

As women who are deeply concerned about the illegal and immoral war in Vietnam, we demand:

that the United States Government bring our husbands, sons, and brothers home now.

that our government recognize and negotiate with the National Liberation Front for the withdrawal of U.S. troops.

self-determination for the Vietnamese people.

that there be open public discussion and debate on the war. As a beginning we demand that Secretary of Defense MacNamara and other government officials testify in public sessions before the Senate Foreign Relations Committee.

that the disciplinary reclassification of the Ann Arbor, Michigan demonstrators be rescinded and that such policies be never again used.

BRING HIM HOME

JOIN THE WOMEN'S MARCH: WED, FEB 23

Women's March Committee
Vietnam Day Committee
2407 Fulton, Berkeley
549-0811

This 1972 leaflet reflects some of the ambiguities of the emerging liberation movement. The form of anti-war protest proposed here is quite moderate—a march ending with the presentation of demands to those in charge of the Oakland, California, induction center, where men were processed for military service. While the protest is organized by women expressing their independence from men, the visual center of the leaflet shows a very tired male soldier. The demonstration is for women only, yet they are encouraged to "dress conservatively, preferably in black," while asking that "the United States Government bring our husbands, sons, and brothers home now."

End the War!
End Our Oppression!

This is the first major anti-war demonstration in which women
have marched together as a unit. We are here today because we
oppose this war that is causing death and destruction both in
Indochina and at home; we demand immediate withdrawal of all
U. S. troops now. We recognize that this war is but one manifestation of a system that oppresses people everywhere on many
levels. *We want not only an end to this war but an end to the
system that is its cause.*

We are marching together as women because this war affects us
as women as well as human beings. As long as resources are
squandered on war, the demands of women's liberation for *free
abortion; free, 24 hour child-care; equal pay, employment and
education* will not be met.

But we didn't have these things before the war and we won't
get them afterwards unless we are organized as a *strong indep-
endant women's liberation movement.*

In order to build such a movement, women's liberation must grow
to include women who face oppression where they work, because of
their race, at home, or because they can't find work.

This movement must demand:

Immediate withdrawal of all U.S. troops from Indochina

Equal pay and employment

Free 24 hour childcare

Free abortion on demand

The Working Women's Committee believes that working women must
play a major role in the women's movement. Being 53% of the
population does not constitute women's power -- our position in
the workforce does. *By organizing on-the-job struggles women
can begin to exercise our collective political power.* If you
want to work with us, if you need help organizing where you
work, or if you want to form a Working Women's Committee where
you live, get in touch with us. Write to:

Working Women's Committee

c/o Sklar
245 West 104th Street
New York, New York 10025

In both the headline and the text, an explicit connection is made between the death and destruction resulting from American military involvement in Vietnam and "a system that oppresses people everywhere on many levels." To address the problems affecting women's economic, social, and health-care circumstances, it is necessary for the United States to pull out of Vietnam immediately so that government funds, personnel, and services can be re-directed toward those issues. Moreover, it is essential for women to organize and advocate politically for and by themselves to demand that their concerns be recognized and acted upon.

WOMEN ARE ALSO AT WAR!

THE WAR TAKES OUR BROTHERS, HUSBANDS, CHILDREN

We are widowed, our children orphaned, our homes wrecked by the Vietnam war--a war which has lost all popular support and profits only a few.

THE WAR TAKES OUR MONEY

As homekeepers, women must carry the burden of inflation. We eat hotdogs for the price of steak. We pay taxes directly to the war every time we buy food, clothing.

THE WAR TAKES OUR SCHOOLS AND HOSPITALS

Nixon puts B-52s before school and hospital buildings. He puts research for napalm before research on cancer. 30,000 students were turned away from California state colleges this fall because the war is robbing funds from the budget for education.

THE WAR TAKES OUR RIGHTS

Black, brown, red, yellow and white--we all strive for decent jobs, for day care centers, for money to feed our children. But we are told to wait for our needs--there is a war going on.

JOIN US - END THIS WAR NOW!

JOIN THE WOMEN'S TASK FORCE

COME TO THE WESTERN REGIONAL ANTI-WAR CONFERENCE

February 28 & March 1

Marina Jr. High School   Fillmore & Bay Streets   San Francisco

Hosted by Bay Area Peace Action Council

Bring ALL the Troops Home NOW!

The early stages of women's struggle for equality and freedom in the 1960s emerged out of the civil rights, Black Power, and anti-war movements, propelled by the radical critique of American society that accompanied them. That context is well represented by the content of this leaflet, likely from the first presidential administration of Richard Nixon. The Vietnam War and its destructive impacts are central to the points listed by the Women's Task Force. Besides killing Vietnamese and Americans, the war is creating burdens for women trying to meet the necessities of everyday life, and robbing them of opportunities for future economic and educational advancement.

WOMEN

The conditions of our daily lives are intolerable. Those of us who work outside of our homes are paid less than men doing the same jobs, and those of us who are black are paid least of all. Few jobs are available to us. They claim that we don't have to support our families, that we don't need as much money as men. That's a lie! From birth we have been told we are the "weaker" sex. Weaker, we work twice as hard and twice as long. Many of us leave work at five to begin work at five-thirty; to feed our families, to clean our houses, to do the laundry, to put our children to bed, and then to collapse ourselves until early the next morning when it begins again. And who does the work in the offices? The male boss, the supervisor, comes in at ten and goes out to lunch at twelve. The women, the secretaries, the receptionists, the file clerks, the "gal friday" do all the work for little pay while the man does his important job for lots of money and lots of prestige. In secret, we give the man our ideas which he presents and gets credit for, sometimes with a little joke about his good old secretary, Mary. Our ideas and our competance are not enough. Without the smile, the cheerful cup of coffee, the sweet good-woman dress and behavior, we are fired. Other important men come into our offices and nod a hello to the "girls": invisible fingers, invisible minds, invisible strength. The only time they see us is when they want to "take" us to bed, and then they only see our bodies. As we get older they see nothing at all.

Those of us who work at home are not paid. We are expected to be grateful for our room and board as were the slaves. We are expected to serve our husbands like slave-masters, the silent helper, the "good" wife. When we try to talk to our husbands they do not hear us. When we yell to make them hear, they tell us we are hysterical, they tell us no one could listen to such an hysterical woman. And then they tell us about the beautiful, young, competant woman in their office, or their friend's smart wife, or their brother's sexy girl friend who never worries,who never "nags". When we meet the other woman we're afraid to open our mouths, afraid we are ugly or dumb or weak or nagging. They have built a wall between us, thick and impenetrable.

Our efforts to join together have been slandered. When we talk they tell us we're gossips. When we move against the outrageous conditions of our lives, they say we are castrating, unfeminine, lazy, stupid, and emotionally sick. And we have only begun to fight our oppression as women.

WOMEN ARE NOT DULL OR PASSIVE OR INFERIOR

WOMEN ARE BRILLIANT AND KNOW HOW TO GET THINGS DONE: AT HOME
                                                         IN OFFICES

MEN IN POWER IGNORE AND LAUGH AT THE WOMEN WHO DO ALL THE WORK

MEN IN POWER ARE DRIVEN BY INSATIABLE GREED AND LUST FOR MORE. THEY HAVE RAPED THE LAND AND WOMEN. THEY HAVE EXPLOITED OTHER MEN. THEY HAVE CREATED A DANGEROUS WORLD OF NUCLEAR WEAPONS, DEATH-TRAP HIGHWAYS, INHUMAN PRISONS, ENDLESS WARS, AND POISONOUS AIR, LAND, AND WATER.

WE ARE NOT SAFE ON THEIR STREETS. AND EVERY STREET IS THEIRS! REVOLUTIONARY FEMINISTS MUST TAKE POWER AND BUILD A NEW SOCIETY!

This is a blunt indictment of the degrading and demeaning ways in which men treat women: "The conditions of our daily lives are intolerable." Women must unite and not allow men to divide and demoralize them. The leaflet claims that male domination has broader destructive consequences, such as the proliferation of nuclear weapons, senseless wars, and environmental abuse. The implication is that with women in positions of influence and authority, such conditions would be reversed: "Revolutionary feminists must take power and build a new society!"

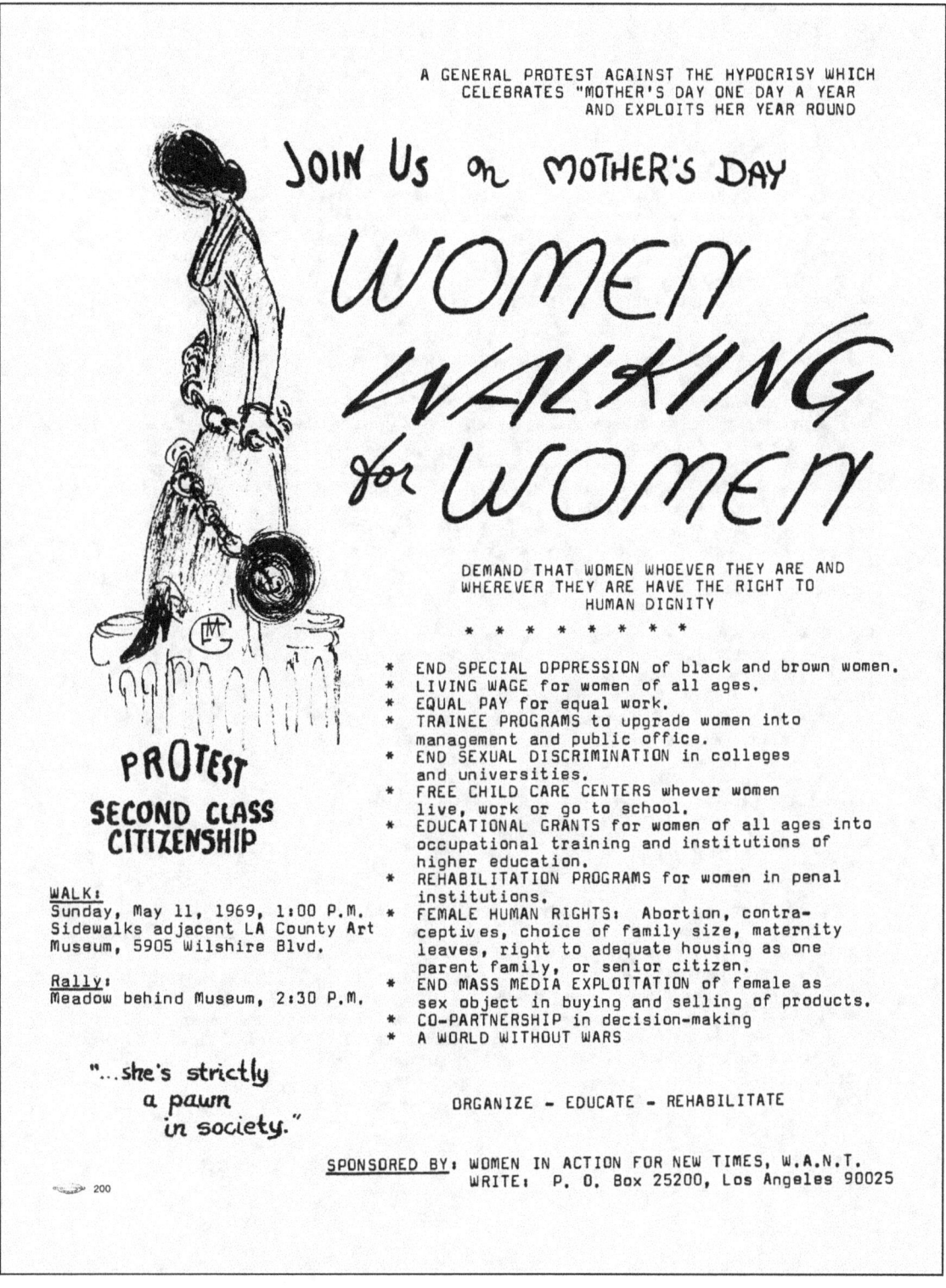

Here is a comprehensive agenda of actions and initiatives that seeks to end the "second class citizenship" of women. "Women walking for women" in protest—by and for themselves and without men involved—expresses the commonality of their oppressive circumstances and the necessity of joining together for political impact. The numerous issues and topics listed suggest that for women to "have the right to human dignity" requires society to undergo major social, economic, and psychological transformations.

LIBERATION IS FULFILLMENT

All women have been oppressed at one time or another. The nature of the oppression has significant common factors such as girls being programmed in school to conform to what society says a girl must be (she can't take industrial arts; she must not get angry or swear; if their is a choice, her brother's college or career takes precedence over hers). Later we are assigned "roles" either by patriarchal church doctrine (think about the marriage ceremony: who gives this woman to this man) or by male dominated psychology. Both systems of thought attempt to exert power over women's minds, to keep them in their places, to diminish their sense of self-worth.

The movement represents the collective efforts of all women to see the nature of oppression from the general point of view and from the personal point of view. The term "raising consciousness" may be defined simply as women coming together to talk about their personal experiences which might include the fact that their grand-mothers had to have abortions furtively. What happens is that we rely on each other in a trusting relationship rather than to pay thousands of dollars to bare our secrets to a "professional". What we have discovered is that we all have classic stories of being brutalized, mishandled, kept down, abused, underpaid, over-worked, unappreciated, and slapped around in a variety of ways, some openly hostile as is society's denial of woman's love for other women; and some terribly subtle ways such as a husband telling a wife she is "over-reacting" or that she is being "emotional".

One of our purposes is to create an atmosphere in which women can see the abuses. Once aware that we are not alone, we begin to care about all women and then to implement effective methods of change. The movement is remarkable because it encompasses a wide variety of dissatisfactions and solutions, ranging from the radicals who distrust all aspects of a system which fosters violence, to women who want clean, safe streets for their children to play in.

Fundamental to the movement is the belief that women have not realized their potential. Liberation is fulfillment, and inherent in the individual's development of potential is the desire and the collective will to see that all women get out from under, that "your grievance is my grievance", that what I want you too may identify with.

I want the right to control my body, its reproduction processes, and that means free abortion on demand. I want 24 hour free day care centers which are community controlled. I want equal job and educational opportunities for women. I want to see more women doctors, lawyers, broadcasters, interviewers, teachers, professors, and university presidents. I want the media to stop exploiting women, to cease the denigration of women in pornographic magazines. I want to see women in plays and movies who are as fine and decent and remarkable as the women I know. I want young women to know that they are valued as people and need not marry to achieve the status they deserve. I want an end to war; clean air and water and parks. I want integrity from public officials half of whom should be women.

ANNE BRADY

This is a remarkable personal statement, portraying the journey a woman through various aspects and stages of her liberation. Although introspective, it is closely connected to the many societal obstacles that limit and constrain women in general. The context of oppression in which women must live also unites them and provides the basis for moving from individual grievance to collective struggle and then empowerment. This first-person account of the evolution of consciousness ends with a vision of a social order where the barriers to equality have been dismantled, and women are experiencing the fruits of freedom.

The Statue of Liberty transformed into a symbol of militant feminism, advertising a discussion of women's liberation at which men are welcome to attend. In 1969, this event at a university during the time that students were arriving for the fall semester was intended to "dis-orient" and challenge them, to raise issues and questions, to move them to critically examine what was considered conventional and normal. After all, shouldn't that be an essential part of a university education?

INTERNATIONAL WOMEN'S DAY

On March 8, 1908, working women in New York City went on strike, to win the right to vote and an end to child labor. In 1910, the International Socialist Congress declared this day a holiday, "International Women's Day." Since that time women have used this day to protest their exploitation and celebrate their struggles.

We know we are not helpless and brainless, even though we're taught to act that way or else. We are never taught about the militant fights women have waged and the struggles we have won when we stick together. Women were in the forefront of the battles against slavery and child labor. Our grandmothers braved the scorn of their husbands, stood up to the cops, went to jail and won the right to vote. We went into the factories and fought for unions to protect us as workers.

In the Phone Company, operators were the main fighting force of the 1947 nationwide strike for recognition of the CWA. Women were militant in many recent wildcats against the phone company and in the 1968 nationwide strike. Last summer, operators in San Francisco and Oakland walked off the board, fed up with the way they are treated. AT&T doesn't give a damn what our lives are like as long as we're passive. We're going to have to band together and struggle hard for what we want.

Women get sold short in all kinds of ways in this society. There aren't enough jobs to go around, the jobs we can get are low paying, there's no child care for our kids while we're at work.

Why are women oppressed? Because it's profitable. If we're used to taking orders at home we're easier to intimidate on the job. If our husbands are hung up about being "the breadwinner," it's easier to get away with paying us lower wages. The Corporations play men and women off against each other to keep everyone's wages down. We are used as a cheap labor force that can be sent back into the home when the corporations don't need us.

Women are getting fed up! We are getting together to take control of our lives. Women's Liberation is fighting for equal wages, child care, birth control and jobs. We are fighting against our oppression on the job, in the home, and in the society. We are fighting for recognition as equal human beings and for a society that is run in the interests of people not profits.

On Sunday, March 8, we are holding an International Women's Day Rally in San Francisco at Dolores Park, Dolores and 18th, at 1 P.M. in solidarity with our sisters here and around the world to celebrate our struggles and advance the fight.

Womens' Liberation   JOIN US!   **union labor donated**

The political revolt by women in the 1960s was a response to the many forms of economic, social, cultural, psychological, and sexual exploitation that they faced on a daily basis. It was nurtured by the frustration that women experienced in seeking to gain "recognition as equal human beings" within the civil rights, Black Power, and anti-war movements. Coming together "in solidarity with our sisters" made for a potent theme on International Women's Day in 1970, an occasion to honor historical struggles and achievements while making it clear that the fight for liberation was far from over. As the leaflet proclaims: "Women are getting fed up!"

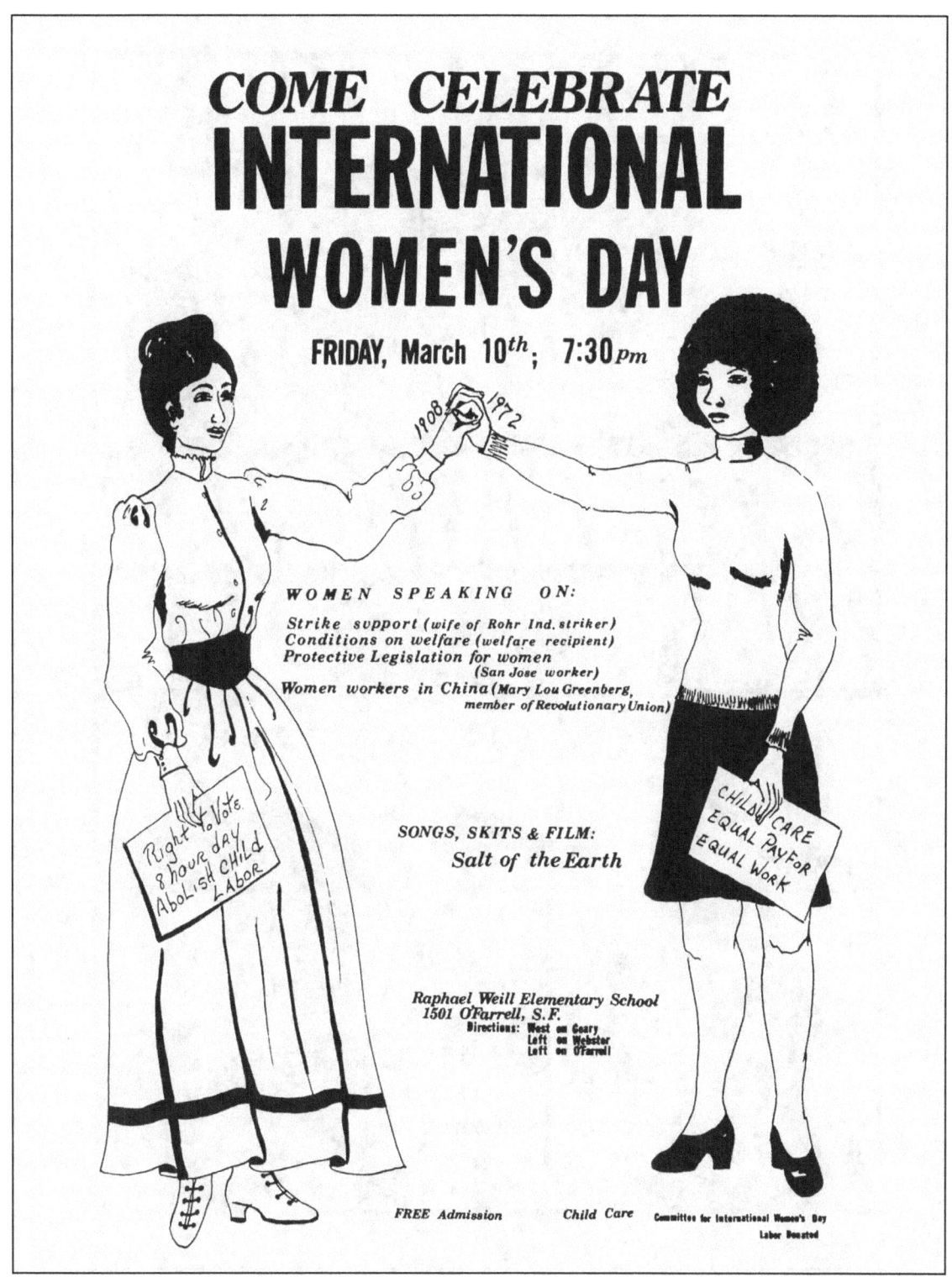

Part of the awakening of feminist independence in the 1960s was the recognition of the contributions made by women's suffrage activism during the early twentieth century, resulting in the 1920 adoption of the Nineteenth Amendment, which established voting rights for women nationally. Continuity with this historical background is portrayed in a 1972 leaflet emphasizing the contentious battle for equality, conducted by women over many decades.

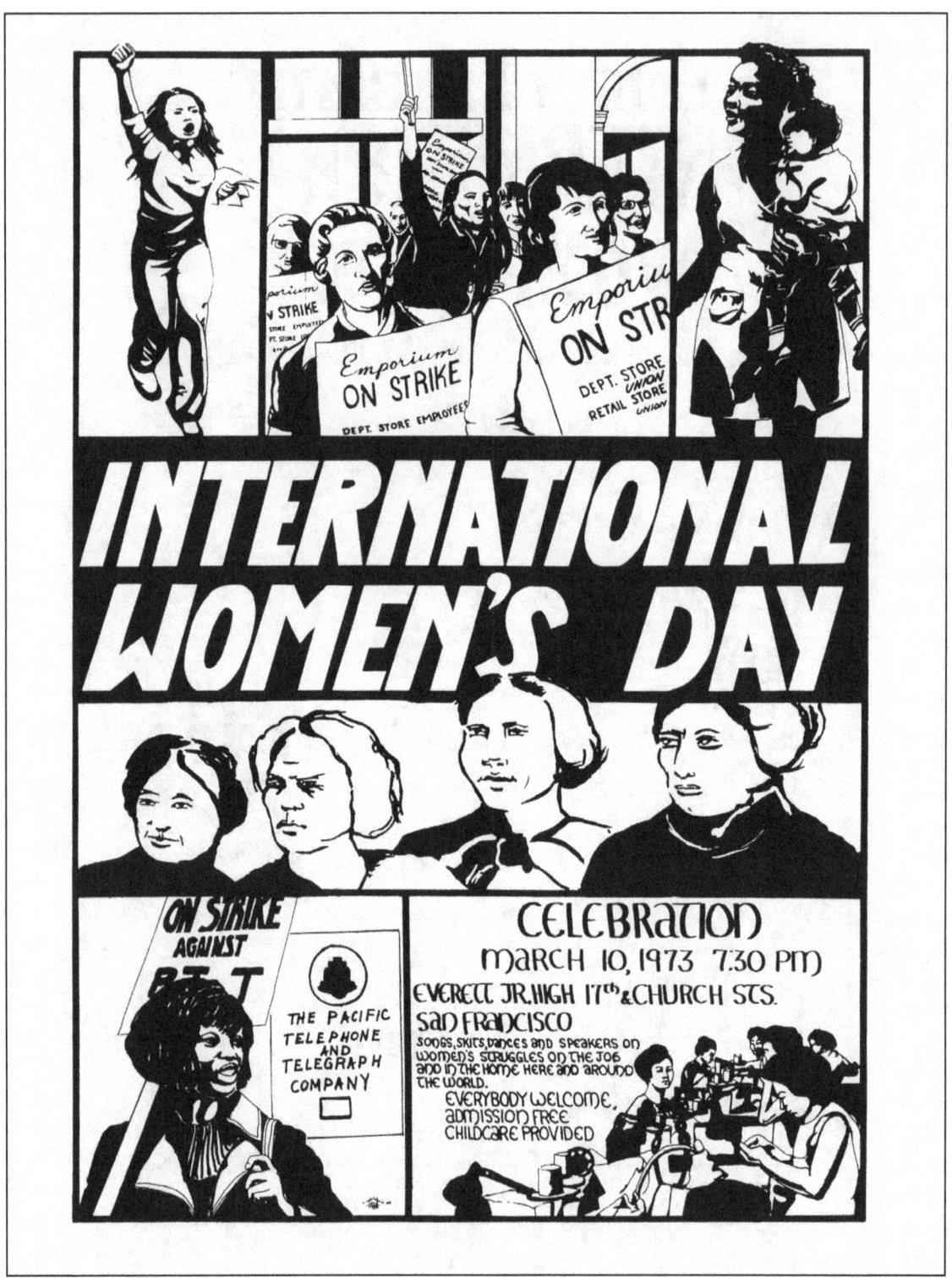

International Women's Day is a cultural and political event that recognizes women around the world and their battle against various forms of discrimination and oppression. These panels show protest scenes with diverse women; based on their appearance and clothing, some of them are women from a previous era, likely the early twentieth century. The focus is on the burden of women's domestic responsibilities and the difficulties that they face seeking employment, themes that have long been part of International Women's Day celebrations.

JOIN THE
WORKING WOMEN'S CONTINGENT
OF
THE WOMEN'S MARCH FOR EQUALITY

WE NEED –
* equal pay
* equal work
* jobs for all women who want them
* quality childcare available to all women

Last year, 50,000 women in New York City marched on August 26.

That march showed people   many for the first time   that women have special needs and that we are fighting for those needs.

It made every local struggle waged by women during the last year   whether for higher wages, abortion law repeal, access to skilled jobs, time-off to care for sick children   *easier*.

Easier because we knew that our *particular* struggle was not an isolated struggle;

Easier because we knew that thousands of women shared our needs;

Easier because our opponents knew it too.

This August 26, we will demonstrate again that our needs and our strength are those of the vast majority of women.

We who have jobs and who are in unions will be playing an even larger role in the women's movement. We must begin to know one another and develop new ways to work together

To begin with, we should march *together* this August 26.

The Working Women's Contingent
at
the south-east corner of
44th Street & 6th Avenue

JOIN US

5:30 p.m. Thursday, August 26

SPONSORS.

THELMA DALEY, *V.P. D65*
ELEANOR TILSON, *Head of Security Plan; RWDSU*
MAE EBERHARDT, *Civil Rights Director, IUE Dist. 3*
JEAN GREENE, *V.P. Local 371 SSEU*
ELEANOR BAILEY, *Manhattan-Bronx Postal Union*
JOAN HVEZDA, *Chapter Chairman, Local 550; ALSSA-TWU*
B. J. BULL, *ALSSA-TWU Local 550*
LILLIAN ROBERTS, *V P DC 37 of AFSCME*

ELEANOR BROWER, *AMC & RSEU*
ROSE FRED LUND, *AMC & RSEU, Chairlady of Women's Division, Huntington*
MARCY PETE, *RWDSU-USW*
JUDY LACOFF, *Local 1199*
CLARA GARCIA, *Cap. Makers Union #2*
VIRGINIA MORTON, *IUE*
JANE HOROWITZ, *ALSSA*

CHARLOTTE MILES, *Local 1199*

Unions listed for identification only.

While the "sisterhood" of women was a unifying force, the women's liberation movement did not have a uniform structure. Similar to the other social movements of the Sixties, women's liberation grew out of many groups and subcultures, which imparted a robust diversity and dynamism. The Working Women's Contingent, with broad sponsorship from labor unions, saw itself as a distinct entity in this 1971 march for equality. Other participants in the women's liberation movement formed around such factors as sexual orientation, political ideology, and ethnic identity.

WOMEN'S LIBERATION and ECOLOGY

The domination of nature by man is the root cause of the
ecological crisis. This idea is implicit in Western thought,
as in Genesis, which states that man has dominion over the
land, the creatures of the sea, air, and land. If this teach-
in is going to help us solve the problems of the environment,
then it must get at the root.

The domination of man over nature has been institutionalized in the American social structure. The basic dynamic underlying dominance is that one builds oneself up by conquering or putting down
another. Thus man feels that he is the center of the universe through his ability
to master the environment and thus the white American male builds his own sense
of superiority by keeping women, blacks and minority groups "in their place."

The liberation of woman from the submissive and inferior position in society
is essential in changing the relationship of man to the environment. Woman's
oppression is seen as her natural state, and is perpetuated by myths that have
origins in primitive society, and by modern psychology. The liberation of woman
involves women demanding control over their lives and bodies, and no longer sub-
mitting to sex-typed roles that have been forced on them.

Woman's main function is as childbearer. Her children become her creations
and she further defines her worth in terms of the quality of those creations. Her
status depends on that of her children. Because her main function in life is
childbearing, woman is not seen as a necessary or equal part of the economic system. She is given the most alienating and low paying jobs.

As long as women are defined as bodies to produce children, we will not
be able to limit the population. Population control is not just a technical
problem, it is a social problem. The solutions to problems of overpopulation
lies in Women's Liberation and in a redistribution of resources. A new identity
for women is needed, one which recognizes her as a complete human being. Childbearing and rearing must be changed from an individual way of life to a social
responsibility. The economic structure must be changed in order to allow women
to create new identities as the present structure only reinforces those roles.
At the same time, more research must be done in the development of safe, easy to
use, effective contraceptives, both for men and women. Free abortions must be
made available to all women who want them.

Women's Liberation is essential in creating a society that can live in
harmony with the environment, and not destroy it. To discuss these and other
ideas, join us in our workshop on Friday night.

Population, Ecology, and Women's Liberation
March 13   Pioneer High School
     10:00   after the panel

Here in the United States, the natural world, as well as women, Blacks, Hispanics, Asians, and Native Americans have all been subject to conquest, exploitation, and domination by White men, with wide-ranging destructive consequences. Liberating women from roles determined by men serves to challenge their pervasive power and influence. Indeed, as this 1970 leaflet asserts, access to both contraception and abortion is an essential part of the process for women to develop new identities as full human beings, which is vital to "creating a society that can live in harmony with the environment, and not destroy it."

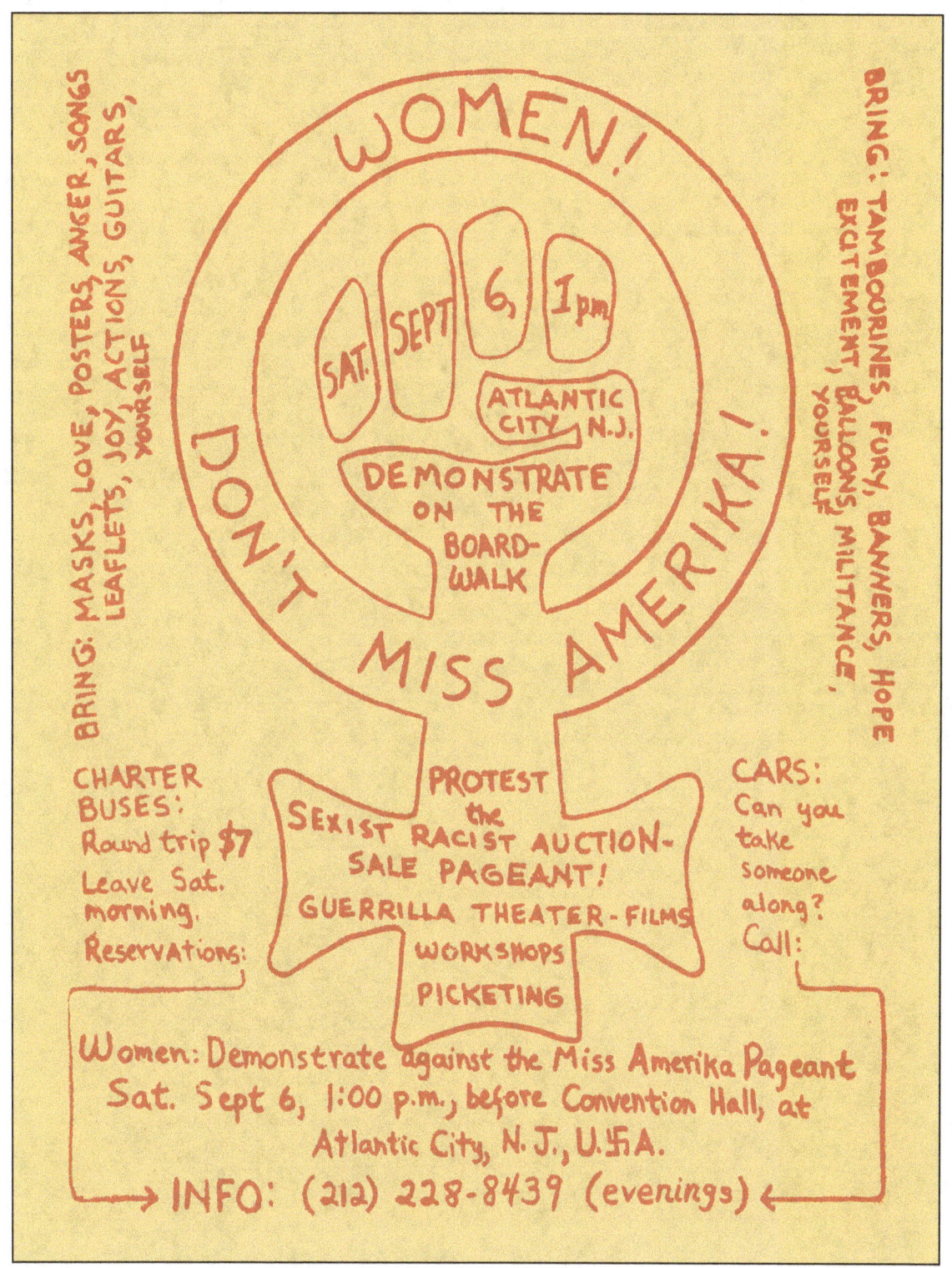

What better way to undermine the traditional Miss America beauty contest than to mount a satirical event combining political and celebratory activities that simultaneously mock and protest the "sexist, racist, auction–sale pageant." Note that the spelling of "Amerika" with a "k" was a deliberate characterization of the United States as a discriminatory society that stereotypes, exploits, and subjugates women. This demonstration against the 1969 version of the Miss America spectacle in Atlantic City, New Jersey, exemplifies the way that politics and the counterculture overlapped during the Sixties, with the latter enlivening and animating the former.

SECTION 5

Gay Rights and Sexual Freedom

EARLY, VERY EARLY, on the morning of June 28, 1969, at the Stonewall Inn on Christopher Street in the western portion of Manhattan's Greenwich Village, it happened. The bar was well known as a gathering place for gay persons, now referred to more broadly by the abbreviation LGBTQ—people who are lesbian, gay, bisexual, transgender, queer. Such establishments were subject to periodic raids by the New York City Police Department. Patrons would typically endure being searched, harassed, intimidated, threatened, arrested. Not on this night, however, not at the Stonewall Inn.

Instead they resisted: they said, "No more"; they said, "We are not ashamed of our sexual orientation"; they said, "You can't push and shove us up against a wall." They pushed and shoved in return; they refused to submit meekly; they fought back; they stood their ground. And as reports of the initial incident circulated throughout the Stonewall Inn neighborhood and Greenwich Village's large gay community, the anger, the unrest, and the defiance grew. For several days, the streets filled with voices saying, "We are not taking it any longer!"

It is not an exaggeration to say that the Stonewall Inn uprising was a major watershed in the history of gay emancipation. Although it is likely an oversimplification to declare that Stonewall "caused" the gay liberation movement, it was certainly essential to its formation, progress, and struggles—which continue today, more than fifty years later.

The unplanned, spontaneous rebellion that started on Christopher Street was an explosive reaction to years of discriminatory, abusive tactics toward gays by the New York police. But it did not occur in a vacuum. By 1969, the historical context of the Sixties had been accelerating for several years. While the LGBTQ status of many may have been hidden, gay people had seen all around them the growing and bolder activism of the movements for civil rights and Black Power, women's liberation, and ethnic identity and solidarity. Homosexual men and lesbian women found common ground with other marginalized groups. These movements were influential in serving as models for gay rights initiatives, as well as for those heterosexuals were also seeking greater sexual freedom by questioning repressive beliefs and traditional behaviors.

What followed Stonewall was the rapid emergence of the gay liberation movement in multiple manifestations—national and local advocacy organizations, a profusion of publications and newspapers, gay pride weeks, gatherings, meetings, manifestos, declarations, statements, political lobbying, legal challenges, and projects to raise awareness—all seeking equal treatment, an end to discrimination, and social acceptance. Demonstrating, shouting slogans, being assertive, fighting back literally and figuratively, refusing to be kept down, were all ways of throwing off stereotypes and finally being truthful. No more shame, no more fear, no more timidity, no more submission, no more self-loathing. For LGBTQ persons, the rejection of cultural prejudices was a powerful step toward self-expression and self-acceptance.

Nationally, it took several decades to recognize the seminal significance of the Stonewall Inn uprising. In February 2000, the site was designated a National Historic Landmark. In June 2016, President Obama announced the Stonewall National Monument, to be managed by the National Park Service. Finally, in June 2019, fifty years after the Stonewall Inn uprising, New York City Police Commissioner James P. O'Neill issued an official apology for the tactics used by police on the night of June 28, 1969.

What united the disparate individuals participating in the various Sixties movements for political, cultural, and social change was the exuberant experience of liberating oneself from persecution and being supported by others who had suffered similar oppression. These movements were pushing to dismantle decades of prejudice so that people could free themselves, individually and collectively, from their marginalized status and live with greater liberty and authenticity. The goal was a historic expansion of the rights and freedoms originally expressed in the Constitution and subsequently delineated more specifically in the Bill of Rights.

The gay liberation movement was in part about acknowledging, accepting, and expressing sexual preferences that were other than strictly heterosexual. In that sense, it was one type of sexual freedom. The Sixties were, though, a period when nearly every form of conventionality was analyzed, questioned, reformulated, or abandoned. With the emphasis on eliminating restraints to freedom, straight people asked why their sexual feelings and behaviors were subject to repression, both socially and legally. Was love a precondition for having enjoyable sexual relations with another man or woman? What about sexual engagement just for pure sensual pleasure? Was there anything wrong with that? Wouldn't it be more sensible to decriminalize prostitution, regulate it, and provide male and female sex workers with periodic medical exams? Why was the meaning of obscenity so closely and almost exclusively connected to sexual acts? What is obscene about the unclothed human body, anyway?

During the Sixties, two common forms of sexual freedom were public nudity and casual sex, or to use a phrase applied by the media of the day, "free love." Both were indelibly linked with the counterculture, a revolt against the constraints and limits of an alienated, materialistic lifestyle dominated by economic definitions of success. A more open attitude toward nudity and sex was a highly publicized part of the counterculture, offering a direct and explicit way to dis-identify with established standards regarding appearance and conduct. Both involved, literally and figuratively, shedding socially imposed norms and attempting to dissolve boundaries between the public realm and private actions.

Countercultural activities such as music concerts, be–ins, happenings, and similar events, planned or not, included smoking marijuana, taking psychedelic drugs, dancing, and instances of nudity, sexual and non-sexual. In these and other ways the counterculture challenged the restrictions and distortions of what was viewed as a destructive political, economic, and social system that engaged in pointless wars, promoted mindless consumption, and damaged Earth's ecosystems.

As part of the counterculture, unrestrained nudity and sex were acts of purification and a celebration of the human form in its natural state. They were about reaching for a more primal, organic life experience unmediated by traditional notions of correctness. Nudity and sex liberated one's personal body while simultaneously turning that liberation into a political statement.

```
        WHAT GAY PEOPLE WANT

1.    We want freedom.  We want power to determine the destiny of
      our gay community.

2.    We want an end to sexism--discrimination because of sex or
      sexual preference.

3.    We want an end to sexploitation--exploitation of our bodies
      by the straight  capitalist, forcing us into prostitution,
      pornography, filth and degradation.

4.    We want decent sex education dealing honestly with the nature
      of our love.

5.    We want decent meeting places for our gay community, a trans-
      formation of the bars, to be democratically run by and for gay
      people.

6.    We want an end to all sexist laws, especially statutes  segre-
      gating us from children and children from us.  We demand gay
      children be removed from the charge of oppressive straight
      parents.

7.    We want an end to the straight portrayal of us.  For too long
      we have accepted that sexist definition.  We will define our-
      selves and our sexual roles.

8.    We want a full inquiry into psychoanalysis.  We challenge its
      validity.  We say that psychanalysis itself is sick.  The so-
      called cure is actually the disease.  We have been railroaded
      into mental hospitals, lured into suicide compulsions and
      obsessions long enough.

9.    We demand public apology and reparations from sexist churches,
      the governments, the communications media and educators.

10.   We want full and open public expression of our love.
```

The sweeping scope of the agenda presented here reflects a strong rejection of the oppression directed toward gay men and women and an exuberant liberation from the repression gays had often inflicted on themselves by subordinating their true identities. The leaflet proudly proclaims: "We want freedom. . . . We will define ourselves and our sexual roles."

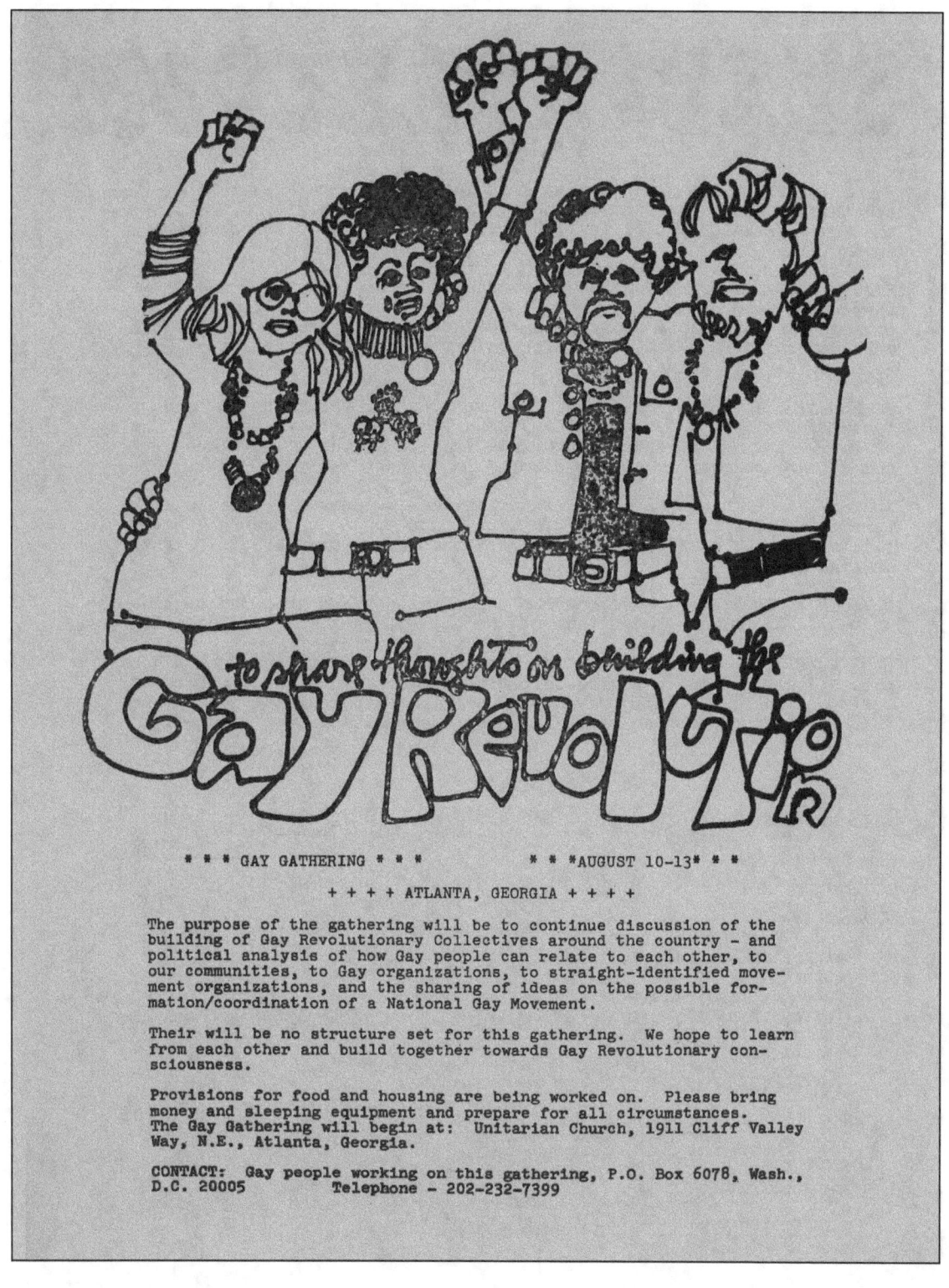

The "Gay Gathering" had an ambitious set of topics to address, including the potential development of a national gay movement, yet paradoxically it emphasized that "There will be no structure set for this gathering." When you are engaged in breaking down stereotypical ideas concerning who and what you are, establishing procedures and protocols for meetings can be seen as limiting the freedom of expression necessary for "revolutionary consciousness" to emerge. It was not unusual during the Sixties for organizations to assert profoundly radical manifestos without accompanying guidelines for their discussion in group settings.

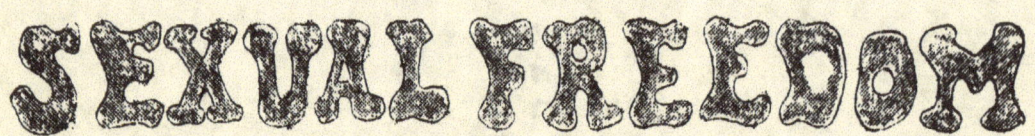

SEXUAL FREEDOM

The SEXUAL FREEDOM LEAGUE of San Francisco is a group of people who join together to defend freedom of choice in everyone's sex life. We believe that no person (or social institution) has the right to force his will on anyone else - neither by rape nor regulation.

SEXUAL EXPRESSION: So long as no choice is imposed by force and no physical damage is done, we believe in complete freedom of sexual expression in any manner whatsoever, whether by one person or by two or more persons, of the same or different sexes, whether married or unmarried. We also favor legalization of prostitution.

PORNOGRAPHY & OBSCENITY: We believe everyone has the right to manufacture, buy, sell, or possess any kind of book, picture, statue, moving picture, etc. We believe in complete freedom of the arts, speech, and communication. We oppose every form of censorship.

YOUTH: We demand repeal of harsh penalties for sexual relations with consenting persons under 18 ("statutory rape"). We oppose college regulations and curfews which restrict the sexual and personal rights of students.

CLOTHING: We believe everyone has the right to wear any kind of clothing in public or private, even that of the opposite sex, or none at all.

CONTRACEPTION & ABORTION: We believe that freedom of choice should be carefully respected in regard to having children, not having children, birth control, and family planning. All laws and hospital regulations which seek to destroy or restrict such freedom should be repealed.

Clip and mail to:
SEXUAL FREEDOM LEAGUE
Box 14007
San Francisco, Calif. 94114

I want to -
( ) Be an active member (by picketing - no dues).
( ) Attend meetings and lectures in San Francisco fairly regularly.
( ) Contribute $_____ toward expenses.
( ) Be an associate member ($1.00 yearly).

NAME:

ADDRESS:
PHONE:

As a frontal assault on boundaries and conventions that prescribed sexual relationships, behavior, and roles, it would be hard to find a better example than this statement, according to which, when it comes to sexual expression, just about every restraint and prohibition should be eliminated in favor of near total personal freedom. This would open up the public realm to all kinds of conduct that was previously private. What had been highly individual choices were instead turned into political declarations. Yet one person's form of sexual liberation might be offensive, distasteful, embarrassing to another. Would that no longer matter?

This simplistic, radical equivalence between being clothed and unclothed betrays sexual biases that persist decades later. The two figures are not daringly explicit; they are intimations of nudity rather than fully developed. And the man is supporting or positioning the woman in a manner that hides him from full frontal exposure. No equality there. Intriguingly, while the leaflet contains few words, it implies basic issues: Can one ever truly be "totally free"? What does it mean to label something or someone obscene or an obscenity? Why are those terms typically associated with sexual imagery or behavior and not, say, war, racism, or the extinction of animal species?

GAY PRIDE WEEK '72
June 17-25

HELLO——DURING THE WEEK OF JUNE 17-25, GAY PEOPLE IN BOSTON WILL CELEBRATE GAY PRIDE WEEK AND THE THIRD ANNIVERSARY OF THE GAY LIBERATION MOVEMENT WHICH GREW OUT OF THE CHRISTOPHER STREET UPRISINGS IN 1969. THOUSANDS OF GAY MEN AND WOMEN THEN TOOK TO THE STREETS IN PROTEST AGAINST CENTURIES OF OPPRESSION; WHEN THE POLICE ATTACKED THEY FOUGHT BACK! THIS IS A TIME FOR US TO COME TOGETHER, MEET NEW PEOPLE, TALK ABOUT OUR PROBLEMS, AND ENJOY OUR LOVE. ALL GAY SISTERS AND BROTHERS ARE INVITED. TELL ALL YOUR FRIENDS.

JUNE 17	JEWISH GAY WORKSHOP
SATURDAY	Our families, our sexuality, our identities as Jews—maybe even our politics as Jews and whatever we can give each other as Jewish gays, at 2 pm 375 Norfolk Street, Cambridge (off Cambridge St. near Inman Square)
JUNE 18	HOMOSEXUALS AND RELIGION (postponed until after Gay Pride Week)
SUNDAY	GAY YOUTH MEET AND MIXER
	Problems we face with our families, our high schools, etc. How can we get together? 5 pm at St. John's Mission Church 33 Bowdoin Street, Boston
	GAY COMMUNAL MEAL (BRING WONDERFUL FOOD TO SHARE)
	7 pm at St. John's Mission Church
	SINGING IN THE RAIN a great musical for free at 9 pm South Station Cinema 23 South Street, Boston
JUNE 19	GAY PEOPLE AND THE LAW, WELFARE
MONDAY	What are the laws? How can we stay out of jail? Welfare for gay people, 74 Joy Street on Beacon Hill at 7:30 pm.
JUNE 20	*MAEDCHEN IN UNIFORM* an excellent 1930's German movie about lesbians in
TUESDAY	a girls' school. FREE at 7:30 pm Charles St. Meeting House 70 Charles St. Boston Followed by men's and women's workshops on their gay relationships
JUNE 21	GAY PEOPLE VS. INSTITUTIONS——PRISONS AND HOSPITALS
WEDNESDAY	What happens to homosexuals in these institutions? What can we do about it? 7:30 pm at Arlington Street Church 355 Boylston Street, Boston
	GAY CANDLE LIGHT MARCH TO THE JAIL
	10:30 March from Arlington St. Church to the Charles St. Jail to support gay prisoners.
JUNE 22	*I WANT WHAT I WANT a film about the changes of a transsexual*
THURSDAY	TRANSVESTITES AND TRANSSEXUALS getting together to talk about our uniquely beautiful life and the problems we face. Other gay people interested will be getting together at the same time to talk about our relationships, gender roles, etc. 7:30 pm at Old West Church 131 Cambridge Street, Boston
JUNE 23	GAY PRIDE WEEK DANCE
FRIDAY	*WOMEN'S BAND* 8:30 pm at Charles Street Meeting House $1.50 Donation.
JUNE 24	GAY PARADE AND RALLY
SATURDAY	1:30 pm the parade begins at Copley Square and will go around the Boston Common with stops at various places (bring beautiful banners and signs and music makers) Rally and Picnic on Boston Common Arts and Crafts Fair (bring your art) Bake Sale WOMEN'S DANCE——SATURDAY NIGHT (more information later)
JUNE 25	GAY PRIDE/CHRISTOPHER STREET CELEBRATION IN NEW YORK CITY
SUNDAY	Buses will be leaving Boston early Sunday morning and returning that night . Tickets $10.

The workshops listed are merely suggestions and will be open to a lot of possibilities. Each night there will be small discussion groups for anyone interested in just talking-- about coming out, problems, questions.

FOR MORE INFORMATION CALL 2621592 days and 492-4489 in the evenings

Everyone Invited

The Stonewall Inn uprising was influential in fostering among sexual minorities the recognition that they shared a history of criminalization, discrimination, and harassment. An early expression of this newly awakened awareness and commonality was Gay Pride Week, and the many facets of gay culture are readily apparent in the agenda for Boston's 1972 event. The realization of community created the possibility of defining a variety of non-binary sexual identities.

Bet you never figured that trying to hold a dance could be a revolutionary act.

Students for **GAY** Power are holding a dance in Pauley Ballroom for the

GAY community _and_ the straight community on May 22. The Administration

is giving SGP a lot of trouble; public **GAY** - ity seems to be a real

irritant. Those of you who have thought about the psychological make-up of

those who feel threatened by **GAYS** know where that's at. The dance

could also play an important role in our getting it together within the

community; it's an opportunity for gays and straights to come together.

GAYS are naturally a part of the struggle against oppression.

A
REVOLUTIONARY
DANCE

"The gay community," as referenced here, likely means both men and women. A dance can be revolutionary when it is an opportunity for gay people to be exactly who and what they are, without restraint, shame, or fear. Such a context means that self-expression becomes a political act, one with deep authenticity because it arises from the person's true identity. There is no question then that "Gays are naturally a part of the struggle against oppression."

CAMPUS SEXUAL FREEDOM FORUM
STATEMENT OF POSITION

The Campus Sexual Freedom Forum is a group of students, faculty and staff of the University of California at Berkeley who join together to defend freedom of choice in everyone's sex life. We believe that no person or social institution has the right to force his will on anyone else -- neither by physical force nor by regulation.

The following is a statement of our stand on certain specific issues.

SEXUAL EXPRESSION

So long as sexual activity is not imposed by force or coersion and no physical damage is done, we believe in complete freedom of sexual expression in any manner whatsoever, whether by one person or by two or more persons, of the same or different sexes, whether married or unmarried.

CONTRACEPTION AND ABORTION

Responsible use of sexual freedom implies that freedom of choice should be carefully respected in regard to having children, not having children, birth control, and family planning. All laws and hospital regulations which seek to restrict or deny such freedom should be repealed. We believe birth control information and supplies should be available to all persons, regardless of age or marital status.

PROSTITUTION

We believe that there should be no legislation against men or women who engage in sexual activity whatsoever; including financial return.

YOUTH

We seek the repeal of harsh penalties for sexual relations with consenting persons under 18 (statutory "rape"). Although we realize no single age can be set at which people will be mature, we recommend 16, the age used by several other states, as being more reasonable. We oppose regulations and curfews in public schools, and in particular at the University, which restrict the sexual and personal rights of students.

CLOTHING

We believe everyone has the right to wear any kind of clothing, in public or private, even that of the opposite sex, or none at all. We recommend this, not to shock or embarrass people, but for its inherent asthetic sake and its comfort.

SEX EDUCATION

We believe that children should be provided with complete sexual education in the primary grades of school.

We do not preach any particular sexual way of life; but rather, seek for each person full freedom to practice any non-coercive sex act.

During the Sixties, just about every aspect of ordinary life was subject to rigorous, relentless examination. This "Statement of Position" proposes to place what conventionally would have been regarded as private behavior—one's sexuality and sexual activity—and move it into the public arena, making it a form of political expression. In this way, the cause of open personal sexuality is linked to other issues and policies related to sex, such as the legalization of abortion, the availability of birth control information and supplies, the legalization of prostitution, lowering the age of consent for sexual relations, and sex education in schools.

FREE PEOPLES PARK
BE NUDE

FOR ONE HOUR, SUNDAY JUNE 4, 2 p.m. to 3 p.m.

BE NUDE in Peoples Park, the park of Free People,
To celebrate life and protest the War.

This invitation extended to all:

Jesus Freaks
Revolutionaries
Mystics
Students
Workers
Street People
Artists   Players
Council Members   Workers   Every Body
U.C. Employees   Rappers
Straights   Loafers
Gays
Violents
Non-Violents
Females
Males
Children
Adults

Be open before the Universe, before your community. Be naked,
with nothing to hide.

If all the world were nude, there would be no more war.
A large number of people taking off their clothes in public would
show our alleged rulers that we will not be intimidated.

Be nude, and say to all the watching world that sex, the life zone,
is worthy to be admired and worshipped--and not bound by clothes.

Be nude, and spread joy to all for what they see in you as a work
of the creator's art.

Be nude, and help a brother or sister who's afraid to be nude.

Be nude, and be both male-liberated and female-liberated in
one freedom afternoon.

BE NUDE FOR ONE HOUR, 2 to 3 p.m. SUNDAY June 4, at Peoples Park,
Bowditch & Haste, Berkeley.

To share in the celebration, bring music, poetry, food, sun lotion.

For more details, be there.

People's Park in Berkeley was created by an eclectic group of people during April and May of 1969 on property owned by the University of California. A manifestation of organic, countercultural spontaneity, it infuriated both the university administration and Governor Ronald Reagan, who ordered the property fenced and the park dismantled. This 1972 leaflet, addressed to a marvelous diversity of individuals, reflects the park's romantic spirit. It proclaims the park as a liberated zone, where nudity becomes a form of protest against the Vietnam War, against death. In "one freedom afternoon," a person can, by being nude, both oppose the war and release repressed sexuality.

GEORGE McGOVERN SAYS <u>YES</u>

HUBERT HUMPHREY SAYS <u>YES</u>

SHIRLEY CHISHOLM SAYS <u>YES</u>

NOW LET'S HEAR THE DEMOCRATIC PARTY SAY <u>YES</u>

<u>YES</u> to a gay rights plank in the 1972 Democratic Platform

Twenty million gay women and men in the United States have
until now been left out of the political process--voters who
until now have had no place to go with their votes; voters who
would work hard for the Democratic party should it become the
champion of their civil rights.

For that's what the gay rights plank is, a civil rights plank.
A pledge to at last give homosexual citizens and taxpayers the
same protections against discrimination in jobs, housing and
public accommodations that the Constitution promises all Americans
and that previous civil rights legislation has guaranteed to
all other groups in our society. A pledge to end the role of
the Federal Government itself as the most blatant discriminator
in America. A pledge to keep our police forces out of the
nation's bedrooms.

It is said that such pledges to ensure the rights of human beings
in our country would sink the Democratic Party in November. But
a refusal by this convention to support equality for a tenth
of its citizens will be an indication to these citizens and
to all men and women of good will that the Party is willing
to sink its own dedication to justice. And it will jeopardize
its chance to win 20,000,000 voters, a bloc which could well
be the deciding vote in the election.

Under our present laws, gay women and men are most often forced
to hide their sexual orientation for fear of being fired or
kicked out of their homes. But gay people don't have to hide
in the privacy of the voting booth. Their votes--and their
hard work for the party in the fall--could provide the crucial
margin of victory.

NATIONAL COALITION OF GAY ORGANIZATIONS--CAMPAIGN '72

The leaflet argues that there are pragmatic, legal, and moral reasons to justify the Democratic Party's adoption of a strong commitment to gay rights in the party platform for the 1972 Presidential election. Existing federal civil rights legislation should be extended to include protection for gay men and women against discriminatory treatment. There must be formal recognition that gay rights are civil rights and thus the concept of equal justice under the law applies to all people, regardless of their sexual orientation. Reducing the stigma attached to being a homosexual or lesbian is consistent with the principles of freedom and liberty upon which the country was founded.

```
THIS IS A CORRECT LINE:

       _____

       It is, by definition, straight.  Which is a drag.

       BITCH is not straight.  BITCH is a non-organization for freaky,
castrating, unlady-like, dope-taking, pinko, joyous, man-hating, un-
puritanical, self-loving, life-digging, dykey, beautiful, angry, uppity,
unrhetorical, anarchistic (and everything else that is the opposite of
straight) women...women who are sick of being screwed by the hip "counter"
culture (or any other culture, for that matter) and want to do something
about it.

       BITCH believes that everyone is sexual --- not heterosexual or
homosexual, just sexual.  BITCH believes that Lilith lives, that God
is a woman, and that the grooviest Marxist was Harpo (because he shut
up and let others get a word in).

       BITCH is tired of being told that acid is counter-revolutionary,
that women are weak or brainwashed, that structure and discipline are
good, that rape is fun, that we must sacrifice for the Revolllshun
(instead of for society?), that we must sacrifice for Our Man, that
we're baby machines, and that we're crazy.

       We're also tired of hearing that if we act like our bitchy selves
we might alienate someone.  We consider every woman's bitchy self is
exactly what needs to be liberated.

       So, if you hate being oppressed by men, society, the "sexual
revolution", and correct-liners, you are probably a BITCH.  Every
woman is, inside.

       If you are, the first BITCH-IN will be

                         Wed. May 27
                         7:30 P.M.
               36 W. 22 St. (between 5th & 6th)

       For more information call SW 5-6668.



                    Remember BITCH IS BEAUTIFUL


P.S. --- Only bitches are bitchy enough to make a feminist revolution.
```

Did BITCH, the non-organization, actually exist? Was the first BITCH-IN really held in Manhattan? This 1970 leaflet is variously nihilistic, whimsical, confrontational, fanciful, and outrageous. There are clear indications it was written by one or more lesbian women. When established roles and expectations that determined relationships between the sexes are obliterated, then feminist anger and rebellion against those oppressive definitions can be released. In this case, what emerges is an alternative female personality expressed as BITCH, which takes joyous delight in being unrestrained, undisciplined, undefined. ("Acid" refers to the psychedelic drug LSD.)

SECTION 6

Ecology and the Environment

Many of those who opposed America's war in Vietnam argued that money and resources should be used to reverse deteriorating living conditions in the United States, including the degradation of environmental quality. Widespread pollution of air, land, and water; excessive materialism and consumerism; and unchecked urbanization and industrialization were scrutinized as a result of this renewed concern about human impacts on the environment. The term "ecology" came to signify the inter-relationships and inter-dependencies among all forms of life. In 1970, the first Earth Day took place and President Richard Nixon signed an executive order establishing the federal Environmental Protection Agency.

There was an interplay between the consciousness expansion of the counterculture; liberation from stereotypes around gender, race, and ethnicity; and the daily televised scenes of devastation in Vietnam. Prevailing myths and preconceptions were shattered—about human awareness and perception, about social biases and prejudices, and about the glory and honor of war. This new cognitive and psychological freedom stimulated a fundamental re-examination of historic attitudes toward nature and the environment. Asking a simple question—"Why are things the way they are?"—led to basic inquiries about the principles that governed society in the United States and other developed nations. Money, jobs, careers, individualism, power, hierarchies, and progress were all seriously questioned.

The countercultural rebellion was influential in the emergence of modern environmentalism in the late 1960s. The counterculture was an expression, in part, of a profound discontent with the emphasis on financial transactions, occupations, and the accumulation of possessions as ways of defining human value and relationships.

The search for deeper and more satisfying meaning in life led many to experiment with powerful psychedelic drugs and to explore non-Western and Native American religious and spiritual practices. This experimentation and exploration resulted in a perspective that viewed living creatures and creations with reverence and respect, that recognized human diversity and unity equivalently. As a consequence, there arose a strong yearning for a simpler, more natural, organic existence that was less competitive, more cooperative and communal, and less oriented to purely personal achievement and status.

The effects of positive experiences with the use of psychedelic drugs dramatically transformed the way people viewed themselves and the world around them, shaking the foundations of their identity. Traditional definitions of identity based on, for example, nationality, ethnicity, religion, family, socio-economic position, geography, and politics, were transcended. Instead, one felt an overwhelming, unmediated, intense connection to every living entity, to "the oneness of being." The result was a dissolution of secular barriers and a sense of self, a notion of citizenship that wasn't determined by terms that differentiated people, but by an inclusive, unifying globalism and membership in a world community.

Women's liberation also played a crucial role in fostering the nascent environmentalism of the Sixties. The rebirth of an assertive but nurturing femininity as the source of human life was embodied in popular ecological references to "Mother Earth." The unique qualities of women and their roles as mothers positioned them to be a moderating influence on male aggression. This became a rationale for female protests against the most horrible form of that aggression at the time—the Vietnam War. Another form of this aggression could be seen in the manipulation of nature as a source of raw materials for manufacturing products by a commercial economy managed largely by White men. In contrast, some believed that women's liberation might help to rebalance the relationship between humans and nature through heightened sensitivity toward, and stewardship of, Mother Earth.

Sixties environmentalism was expressed using romantic, transcendental language as well as through phrases that were confrontational and uncompromising, an amalgam that reflected the impact of the anti-war movement, political radicalism, and the counterculture. Those influences are apparent in the language and phrases from the leaflets in this section, for example:

- Since Americans consume more per capita than any other country we have the worst impact on the planet's support system;
- The earth is finite, greed is infinite, profit is theft;
- All of us on this planet, this life raft we call Earth, will make it together or we won't make it at all;
- No nation has the right to build atom bombs, or use napalm, or pollute the air we all breathe, or the water we all drink;
- Stay high with nature;
- In this era it is possible for all living and non-living things to live peaceably together; and

♦ A new age has come and our survival depends upon creating a balanced ecological system for ourselves on the Earth.

The ecological awareness of the Sixties confronted a pragmatic challenge: how to reverse decades of environmental imperialism, domination, subjugation, exploitation, and destruction. Over the ensuing years, that challenge has been met by a combination of activist and advocacy organizations, technological innovation, and government bureaucracies at all levels. There remains, however, a paradox: environmentalism is animated by a holistic perspective emphasizing the interconnectivity of all life forms, yet its progress is measured incrementally, by the many specialized, separate technical disciplines that have developed to address a multi-faceted environmental crisis.

... a movement emphasizing individual action and personal ethics, not a
    formal organization.

... creating new life styles to reduce the waste and destruction of our environment.
    Since Americans consume more, per capita, than any other country we have the
    worst impact on the planet's life support system.

... using biodegradable soaps and cleaners or none at all.

... not taking a bath every day (unless you are dirty or stink).

... putting bricks in your toilet tank to conserve water when flushing.

... not using DDT and other pesticides with long residual effects.

... using natural predators -- not pesticides.

... recycling wastes -- paper, glass, aluminum (contact Tom Regan c/o Ecology Action
    Education Institute).

... refusing to buy products in non-returnable/reusable containers.

... growing your own.

... keeping a compost heap of grass and garden clippings and biodegradable
    garbage in your yard. No need to buy fertilizers.

... to begin or tend a park.

... requesting a free tree from the city for your yard (in Berkeley call 841-0200).

... being vocal about waste and pollution. Write or phone those responsible and
    those charged with our protection. And keep informed.

... sponsoring neighborhood cleanups.

... fighting those individuals and companies which profit by the sale, use, or
    manufacture of products which are harmful to the ecological system or deplete
    natural resources. The earth is finite -- greed is infinite; profit is theft.

... voluntary birth control, abortions, and incentive programs for family limitation
    and planning.

... grass roots survival education.

... not driving a car (use and improve public transportation and smog free locomotion).

... finding a project related to our survival and doing it; working alone or
    with others.

... supporting the Ecology Action Education Institute which exists totally by
    donations of your time and/or money.

For more ideas and information on specific projects contact:

Ecology Action Education Institute   Box 9334 Berkeley, Calif. 94709

Berkeley's Ecology Action Education Institute linked the damage caused by America's war in Vietnam with environmental degradation here at home. Both were viewed as resulting from a common cause: profound disregard for human life and the natural world. Some activists became frustrated with the continuing expansion of the conflict and turned their attention to local environmental projects whose beneficial impacts were practical and visible. Hence the orientation to "individual action and personal ethics." The specific conservation activities on the Ecology Action list still remain relevant today, more than fifty years after they were originally written.

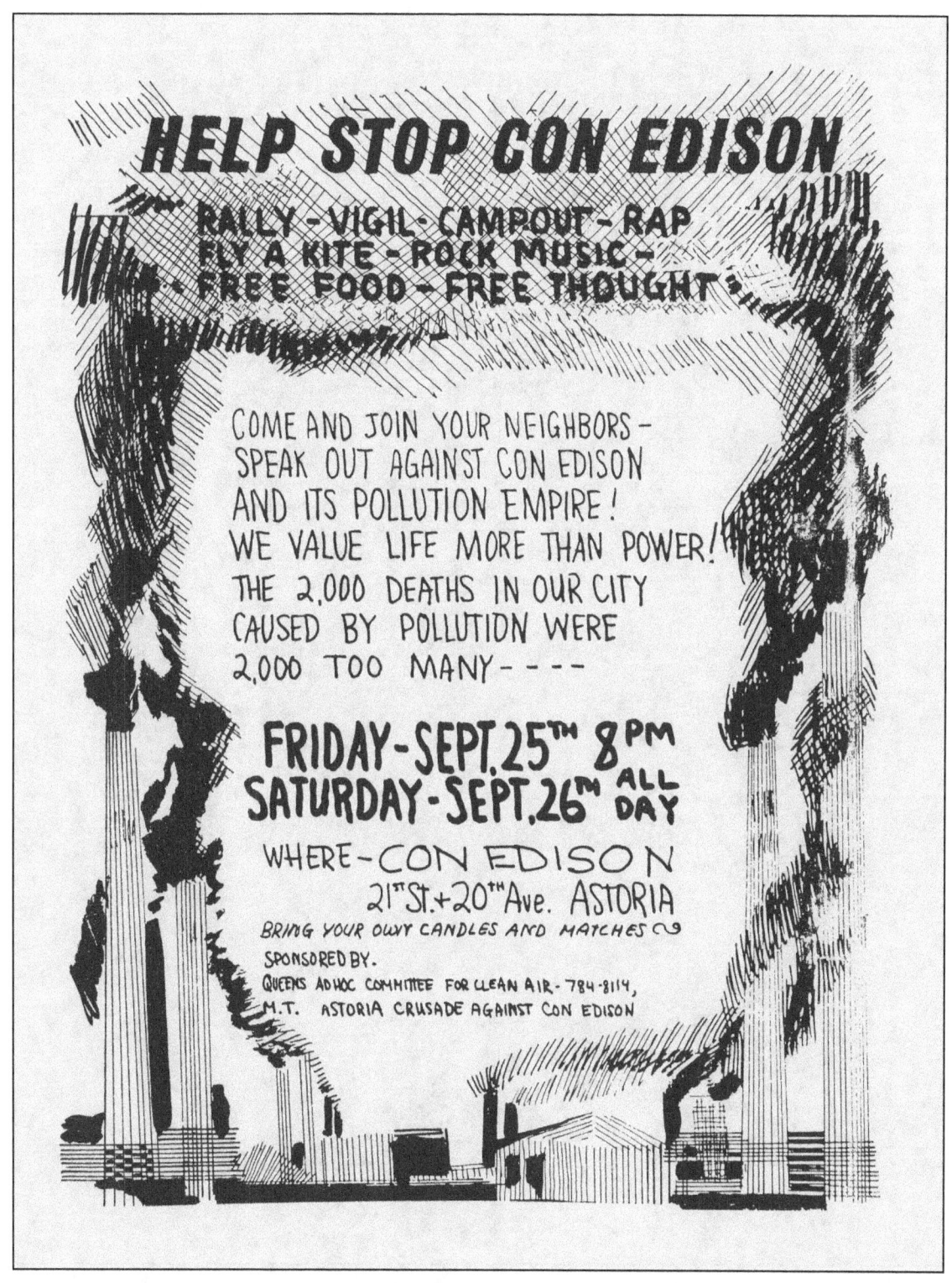

Consolidated Edison, Inc., also known as Con Edison or Con Ed, is an energy company that delivers electricity, gas, and steam to New York City and Westchester County. This 1970 rally and vigil was to protest air pollution from Con Edison's power generation operations. There was a counter-cultural component accompanying the political event, as was often the case during the Sixties. (Astoria is a neighborhood in the Borough of Queens, New York City.)

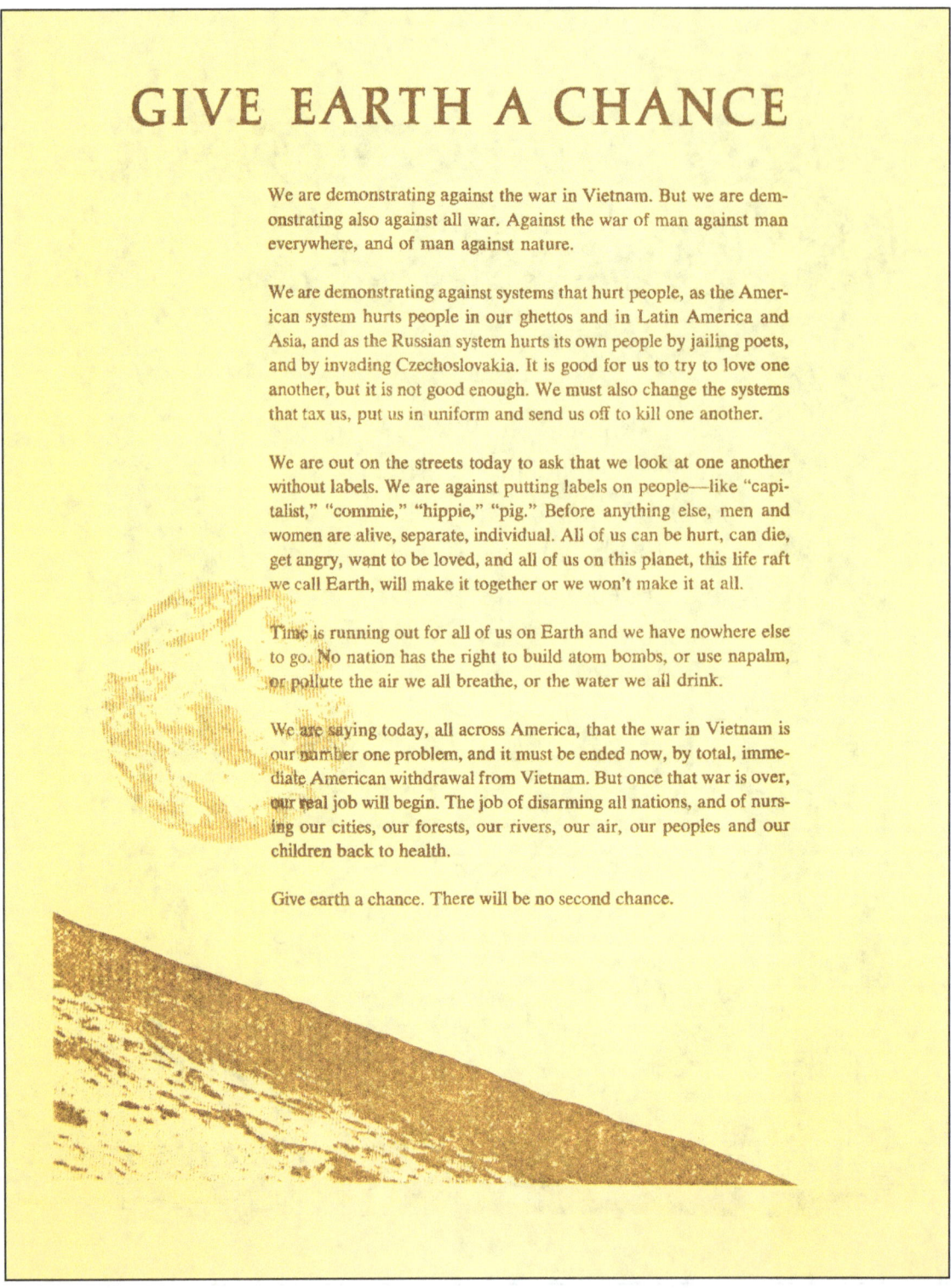

GIVE EARTH A CHANCE

We are demonstrating against the war in Vietnam. But we are demonstrating also against all war. Against the war of man against man everywhere, and of man against nature.

We are demonstrating against systems that hurt people, as the American system hurts people in our ghettos and in Latin America and Asia, and as the Russian system hurts its own people by jailing poets, and by invading Czechoslovakia. It is good for us to try to love one another, but it is not good enough. We must also change the systems that tax us, put us in uniform and send us off to kill one another.

We are out on the streets today to ask that we look at one another without labels. We are against putting labels on people—like "capitalist," "commie," "hippie," "pig." Before anything else, men and women are alive, separate, individual. All of us can be hurt, can die, get angry, want to be loved, and all of us on this planet, this life raft we call Earth, will make it together or we won't make it at all.

Time is running out for all of us on Earth and we have nowhere else to go. No nation has the right to build atom bombs, or use napalm, or pollute the air we all breathe, or the water we all drink.

We are saying today, all across America, that the war in Vietnam is our number one problem, and it must be ended now, by total, immediate American withdrawal from Vietnam. But once that war is over, our real job will begin. The job of disarming all nations, and of nursing our cities, our forests, our rivers, our air, our peoples and our children back to health.

Give earth a chance. There will be no second chance.

A clear message is conveyed in this text, that the destruction and death inflicted by the American intervention in Vietnam are part of the broader environmental devastation on Earth caused by human pollution. Ending that intervention is directly connected to the achievement of systemic political change—supporting universal disarmament and dedicating resources to restoring and sustaining essential ecosystems.

This page of "stamps" offers messages about the environmental movement overlapping with the Sixties counterculture—psychedelic drug experiences that heightened consciousness of the connections between humans, animals, and nature; dissatisfaction with the shallowness of occupational roles; rejection of a lifestyle defined by consumerism and materialism; grappling with environmental degradation; opposition to America's militarism in Vietnam. (The Haight-Ashbury, a San Francisco neighborhood, was a center of countercultural experimentation during the Sixties. The Summer of Love, a celebration of that experimentation, was actually in 1967.)

What's happening on Earth Day?

The streets belong to the people!

ON FIFTH AVE. FROM 59th ST. TO 14th ST.
(FROM 12-2 P.M.) YOU'LL FIND PEOPLE, NOT TRAFFIC!
Be one of them! Walk...bicycle...roller skate...enjoy!

You'll also find:
Kurt Vonnegut Jr. , and other authors, at the 42nd St. Library at noon.
The Voices of East Harlem.
A Baroque Brass Ensemble at St. Patrick's Cathedral and more!

ALL TRAFFIC BANNED ON 14th ST. FROM 2nd AVE. TO 7th AVE. FROM NOON TO MIDNIGHT.

A giant exposition of 75 exhibits!
A panoramic view of environmental problems and some surprising solutions.

And an exciting program from noon to midnight in Union Square!

PETE SEEGER	MARGARET MEAD	JERRY ORBACH	TOM PAXTON
MAYOR LINDSAY	HERMAN BADILLO	LEONARD BERNSTEIN	JEROME KRETCHMER
PAUL NEWMAN	OSCAR BROWN JR.	THOMAS HOVING	DENNIS HAYES
ARTHUR GODFREY	BROTHER KIRKPATRICK	CAST OF HAIR	ED KOCH
ODETTA	GARRY MOORE	BESS MYERSON GRANT	Plus many others!

Watch films projected on the sides of buildings.
Imagine living in a geodesic dome.
Participate in an environmental sculpture happening.
Bring non-returnable bottles to a surprise event.
Breathe inside a "fresh-air bubble".
Find out if your neighborhood supermarket sells fruit covered with pesticides.
See street singers, dancers, and theater groups.
Take an eye-opening tour of our waterfront and subways.
Talk with conservation groups, city agencies, corporate representatives and community
leaders about your own local environmental problems.
Help plant a tree.

Find out what you can do to help fight pollution, crowding, noise,
garbage, rats and lead poisoning right here in New York.

COME ON FOOT, BICYCLE, POGO STICK OR SKATES...BUT LEAVE YOUR CAR AT HOME!

A series of diverse activities celebrating what was likely the first Earth Day (April 22, 1970) were scheduled to take place in Manhattan. Featured participants included politicians (Mayor John Lindsay, Herman Badillo, Ed Koch), musicians (Pete Seeger, Odetta, Oscar Brown Jr.), and actors (Paul Newman, Jerry Orbach), as well as Margaret Mead, anthropologist; Leonard Bernstein, orchestra conductor; and Dennis Hayes, one of the chief organizers of Earth Day. The event intended to raise awareness of environmental issues and strategies but was also a countercultural "happening" with some levity: "Come on foot, bicycle, pogo stick, or skates . . . but leave your car at home!"

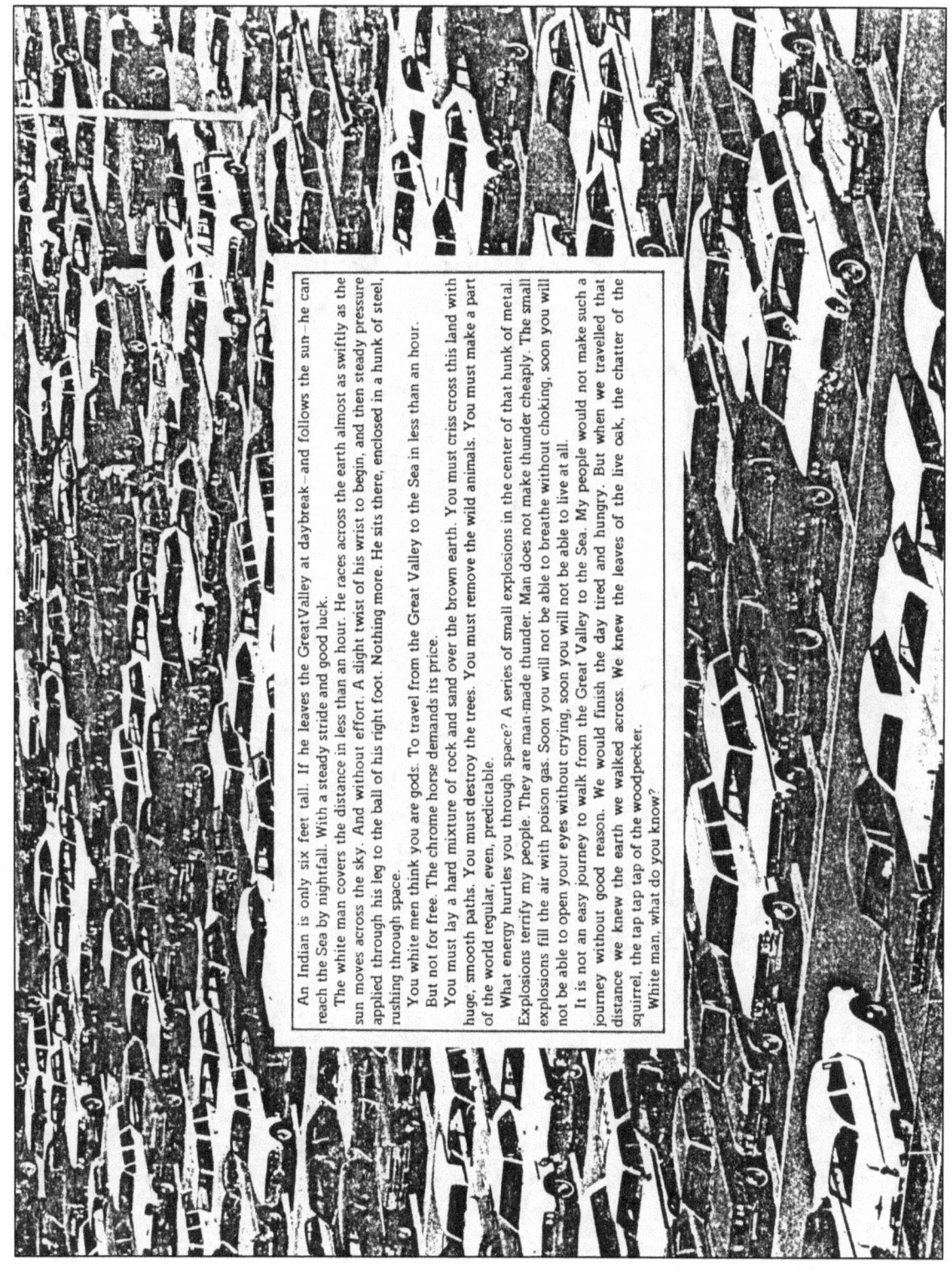

Do the phrases "white men" and "white man" mean all White people or just males? Are White women viewed as less environmentally arrogant and destructive by the author(s) of the leaflet? Who wrote the leaflet and what motivated such a harsh contrast between how an "Indian" and a "white man" travel across and impact the landscape? Even without providing answers to these questions, the power of the leaflet's content is undeniable.

In this age it is possible for all living and non-living things to live peaceably together.

STUDENTS FOR NEW AGE UNIFICATION will sponsor an ecological presentation, involving music, slides, light show, and readings, tracing man's changing relationship to earth.

Underlying all is the basic question which must be answered: "What is the ideal relationship between man and his environment?"

COME, SHARE, RAP — Food and Drink, Free.
FRIDAY   8:00 P.M.
MAY 1, 1970   TAN OAK ROOM
                    4th FLOOR, STUDENT UNION

The event promoted here took place shortly after the first Earth Day. The name of the sponsoring group—Students for New Age Unification—reflects the desire to achieve a more balanced relationship between humans and the natural world. The drawings display a romantic innocence that is in stark contrast to the serious topics proposed for discussion: "man's changing relationship to earth" and " the ideal relationship between man and his environment." The leaflet does not offer an agenda for action; instead, it is an invitation to a philosophical exchange, to "come, share, rap."

 **GROWTH**

We have a lot to do in the next few years if man is to survive.
The key problem is overpopulation.

In order to live, we have to obtain certain things from the Earth. In order to have meaningful, happy lives, we have to preserve the quality of our environment. We have already suffered irretrievable losses. No matter what we do now, no matter how wise we are, there will be great future losses.

The only long-range solution is population stability.

---

ecology

Ecology is a field that has to do with the relationships between living things and their environment.

An ecological point of view is a new way of looking at the world, with man inseparable from his surroundings. This way does not come easily to us, for throughout most of western civilization the emphasis has been on man against nature. This old way of looking at things no longer works. Our past mistakes have caught up with us.

A new age has come and our survival depends upon creating a balanced ecological system for ourselves on the Earth.

---

some population-related problems

POLLUTION:
Air: smog, noise, fallout
Water: sewage, thermal, industrial
Land: garbage, litter, junkyards, mining, roads
Biological Systems: pesticides, bio-active chemicals, radioactivity
CROWDING:
Tension
Indifference—cheapening of life
Jams—traffic, airways
Blight—slums
Crime
Congested parks
SHORTAGES:
Minerals
Energy—oil, gas, coal, uranium

Water
Land—open space, forests, agriculture, recreation
FACILITIES:
Food
Housing
Schools—higher education
Hospitals—medical care
Services—fire, police, courts
Cultural
Transportation—highways, mass transit, airports
QUALITY OF LIFE:
Space—hiking, thinking
Quiet
Wilderness—wildlife
Individuality

Zero Population Growth viewed unchecked population growth as the primary cause of a multitude of negative environmental, social, economic, cultural, and psychological conditions afflicting people around the world. ZPG argued not only for measures to control population, but for the development of an ecological consciousness that would transform and re-balance the relationship between humans and nature to reverse the destructive impacts imposed on the natural world.

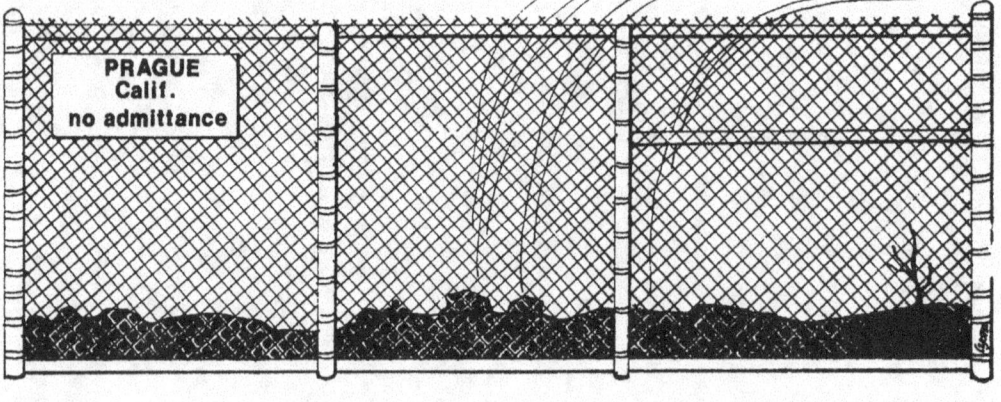

JOIN THE STRUGGLE FOR THE PEOPLE'S PARK
COME TO BERKELEY FRIDAY MAY 30, MEMORIAL DAY
WE WILL MARCH TO OUR PARK --TO THE PEOPLE'S PARK
WE WILL DEMAND THAT THE FENCE COME DOWN

We have been in the streets since they put the fence up. The park represents our attempt to build an enclave of beauty, joy, and humanity, in an increasingly polluted, dismal, rigid, repressive society. Their decision to destroy, to fence in our park, reflects the very essence of this decadent social order. The People's Park has become an issue of statewide, national, and international concern. This did not occur merely because the state did us an injustice. Uncounted injustices occur every day and pass by unnoticed.

Our support, and the victory we expect to win, grow out of our willingness to fight back. We are fighting to return our park to the control of the people in the community--the people who built it. The one thing those in power fear is people who get together and fight in their interest--people who are unwilling to accept the arbitrary authority of the state. The black movement, the student movement, the anti-war movement have begun to resurrect the great American tradition of fighting back. The tradition is spreading. COME TO THE MARCH.

The police, the national guard, the shooting, the teargas, the helicopters, the state of emergency, the curfew, the arrests, the beatings, the harassment, the blanket of terror that has been thrown over Berkeley--this is their response to people in motion. The good people are outraged. But unless the police are disarmed, unless the police mutual aid pact is revoked, unless the military is kept out of civic affairs, unless the ability to revoke all civil liberties by declaring a state of emergency is destroyed, the events of the past weeks will recur, not only in Berkeley, but throughout the land. The state possesses and is committed to maintaining a virtual monopoly on violence--its police, armies, and jails. It is on the basis of these that it exercises its will, that it protects the interests to which it is beholden. Violence will ultimately be eradicated when and only when oppression and the state's complicity in its maintenance are eradicated. We do not seek violence. When it occurs, we are its major victim . But we will not permit our lives to be governed by fear and intimidation. COME TO THE MARCH***DEMAND THE FENCE COME DOWN***THE PEOPLE'S PARK MUST BE RETURNED TO THE PEOPLE.

People's Park (see page 119) combined Sixties political activism with countercultural celebration. When Governor Ronald Reagan and the university administration closed the park and fenced the land, a confrontation between protesters and law enforcement led to Reagan sending in the National Guard. This peaceful march was in response. People's Park raised fundamental issues: the validity of property ownership; the environmental responsibilities of powerful institutions; the role of community participation in land-use decisions. (The "Prague" reference links People's Park with Czechoslovakia's 1968 liberalization movement, ended by the Soviet Union's military intervention.)

The Nixon Administration proposed construction of the Three Sisters Bridge over the Potomac River, which would link several highways and produce a direct connection between Virginia and Washington, D.C. Vehement opposition arose from community and neighborhood groups across the economic spectrum. Issues in the controversy surrounding the bridge included its environmental impact, urban preservation, inner-city integrity, the power of the federal government, and the District of Columbia's lack of political influence. There were protests at the construction site in 1969. Legal challenges halted the project, and in 1972 the effort to build the bridge ended.

SECTION 7

The Counterculture

A Genuine But Conflicted Revolt

THE CULTURAL REBELLION OF THE SIXTIES involved primarily White youth, and was expressed through the use of psychedelic and hallucinogenic drugs, clothing styles, communal living, rock-music concerts and festivals, sexual liberation, exploration of non-Western religious and spiritual practices, re-establishment of a primal connection to Mother Earth, and deep discontent with occupational roles. To a certain extent, the counterculture was a rejection of political activism and emphasized that a "New Age" would evolve from the pursuit of alternative lifestyles as the existing social order collapsed. At its best, the counterculture, even though fleeting, was a positive life force responding to the death machine unleashed by the American military in Vietnam.

Beyond this brief summary, the counterculture was . . .

- ♦ The sounds and voices of those trapped beneath and within the foundation of modern America as it slowly, then more quickly, began to crack;

- ♦ The stresses and strains of that cracking;

- ♦ The meanderings and wanderings of linear mentalities as they coped with multi-dimensional explosions, implosions, and stimulations;

- ♦ Logical organization giving way to experiential knowledge;

- ♦ The distinction between inner life and outer life crumbling under a wave of organic unity, with this dissolution of the artificial distinction between external and internal undermining schemes previously used to assign meaning and order to human experience;

- ♦ The realization that an essential step toward accessing eternal realities and realms, toward beginning the process of cognitive expansion, required detaching from the visible, everyday world that crushed in on one's mind and senses from all sides;

♦ The awareness that what was commonly considered "sane and rational" was deeply and profoundly not that at all; and

♦ An avalanche of thoughts, emotions, and statements in underground publications and books; on walls, posters, and buttons; in music, dance, and art; and spoken during gatherings and demonstrations, all proclaiming by their very form and existence:

We are natural creatures

NO MORE WAR

Freedom from oppression, both physical and psychological

People, not personnel

Experience BE-ing

We are ONE.

The dilemma became how to keep what originated as a transformation in consciousness from being reduced to the block letters of a newspaper headline or the trinkets and curios available at the local "head shop."

Not long after its birth, the authentic social revolution called "the counterculture"—itself an unfolding process—was turned into a product to be bought and sold, brightly packaged in many different ways and available to gullible, hungry souls eager for something to hang onto. So many people clutching fervently to a fragile experiment perhaps led to its early demise. A creation submerged and doomed by the overwhelming weight of the need for it—consumed, literally, by the decay it emerged from originally.

In its abandonment of the "straight" world, which was governed by social rigidity, financial transactions, and sensual repression, the counterculture represented wide-open possibilities and ideals. While there was little doubt as to what was being rejected, the counterculture was an evolving rebellion, its future directions unclear. So the space it occupied overflowed with the tensions and contradictions inherent to pivotal, historical turning points. The shedding of conventional identities and the development of new ones wasn't a clean, surgical process. It proceeded in fits and starts. Some of the baggage from the past carried forward into an unknown future out of habit and the need for stability. All the while, those involved with this evolution were trying to figure out "Who and What Am I?"

This was the iconic manifestation of the counterculture: young people with flowing hair, serene faces, hands uplifted toward the sky, bodies in motion with ancient rhythms while wearing the clothing of Native Americans, with innocent smiles and blazing eyes, and the holy potion of marijuana offered as a universal sacrament—all enacted under a canopy of music that enveloped the entire scene so that each person and element lost its distinct shape and flowed together, forming a vibrant collage of human energy that moved inward, then outward, continuously in motion.

The Gathering of the Tribes for a Human Be-In

THE PUREST COUNTERCULTURAL SCENE that I experienced was "The Gathering of the Tribes for a Human Be-In" at the Polo Field in San Francisco's Golden Gate Park on January 14, 1967. A leaflet announcing the event said, "Bring food to share; bring flowers, beads, costumes, feathers, bells, cymbals, flags." Several years later, I wrote this remembrance of, and reflection on, the Gathering of the Tribes:

With almost childish, giddy anticipation and exhilaration, my friends and I made our way toward the Polo Field in Golden Gate Park. For a few minutes we were our own unique group, but we quickly began merging with others who, it seemed, were moving intently to revitalize a dormant piece of earth just by the sheer momentum and vitality of our presence. Like huge, pulsating veins flowing to the heart, we were all converging on the same point. Converging? No, more like skipping, running, jumping, prancing, dancing, floating, gliding, as if drawn by a gentle magnet to be together for a while.

People were streaming down through groves of trees into the basin of the Polo Field. What jolted me like a ZAP of electricity interrupting a daydream was the sudden appearance of thousands of free-e-e-eaks, each of them having traveled their own individual paths over the past three or four years, away from American normality and conformism into diverse, uncharted journeys and frontiers.

I stopped for a moment to observe the ebbing back and forth, the swirling mass of faces and bodies undulating like different parts of a single organism. The distance dulled sound, and I stood on a small knoll, mesmerized by what was unfolding— a wave of humanity swaying, surging, swirling.

The whole panorama seemed suspended in time, like a field of tall grass slowly blowing in the wind. What a phantasmagoria of sight, smell, voices, music. It was as if from the bowels of a deadened, decaying society a blasting, bursting, bubbling sensory show had been born . . .

. . . with beads and bells and flowers in their hair haIR HAIR! and flags and placards and bandannas and boots and HAIR! and painted faces and stovepipe hats and sequined cheeks and foreheads with colored splashes and dots of green, yellow, blue, covering bodies that seemed to glow and radiate in the afternoon light . . .

. . . and robes, gowns, earrings of every shape/size/length dangling, chiming, accentuating graceful, sloping necks . . .

. . . and then bands playing and people dancing alone or in groups, with marijuana smoke rising slowly over the Polo Field.

None of these occurred as separate actions, but all melded together, overlapping in a continually changing kaleidoscope, a celebration and display of an emerging counterculture: hopeful, open, searching.

The Gathering of the Tribes was intended to help foster a reconciliation between those who would change America with ideas, discussions, demonstrations, and confrontations, and those who would encounter each other and themselves, take psychedelic drugs, reunite with nature, and explore internal dimensions. Beyond this oversimplified dichotomy were the many thousands who were stretched tensely and vulnerably between all manner of combinations and variations of these two different but overlapping pathways. For the political and cultural explorations of the Sixties were always in flux: moving, weaving together, then going in separate directions, then crossing each other again.

Yet, sadly, the countercultural spirit contained within its joy and freshness the roots of deterioration and demise, for the bringing forth of an alternative lifestyle outside conventional behavior exposed that vulnerable spirit to distortion, corruption, and commercialization. In moving out from its points of origin, the various facets of the cultural rebellion collided with harder, more caustic realities, producing strange hybrids and conflicting actions such as talking about the revelations of heightened awareness one hour, then becoming so stoned and obliterated that what was said sounded like a broken tape recording gone berserk. Then there was criticizing the accumulation of gadgets and material possessions, yet eagerly buying posters, hash pipes, beads, bells, colorful shirts, incense, body oils, black lights, albums, and countless other items offered by American capitalism to the "youth market." Paradoxes like espousing the value of "deep communication," while at the same time not being able to hear what another person was saying because the room was being inundated by the reverberations from an expensive stereo system—besides which, that person had a headset on to amplify the music.

And more sinister developments were evident. Within a short span of time, the chemical substances that were often given out freely at music concerts, dances, and spontaneous happenings to stimulate mental freedom became the focus of intense competition among pushers, gangs, and assorted thugs, resulting in beatings and muggings. Even murder. San Francisco's Haight-Ashbury neighborhood, once viewed as the center of "Flower Power," degenerated into a kind of Skid Row for downtrodden rebels who, unable to escape into the countrysides of Northern California or Oregon, or to find shelter in any safer, saner location, instead crouched, huddled, and hovered in doorways, hallways, and alleys — dazed, confused, and wondering, like the rest of us, what in God's name had happened.

The Synthesis

The countercultural rebellion has been characterized in a such a way as to distinguish it from the more overtly political initiatives of the Sixties. The counterculture was associated with the music of the period, the use of drugs to alter consciousness, discontent with defining life according to work roles and economic success, resurrecting a simpler lifestyle closer in harmony with nature's organic processes, and pursuing more authentic human relationships not defined by or limited by traditional norms and boundaries. In contrast, the multidirectional political activism of the 1960s occurred expressly in the public arena: vigorously opposing America's war in Vietnam; battling on many levels for extending equality, justice, and freedom to people who were oppressed and marginalized based on their race, ethnic heritage, gender, or sexual preferences; and advocating for a profound recognition of our involvement with, and dependence on, an intricate web of ecological relationships, thus offering an alternative to continued human domination and exploitation of the environment.

A more realistic perspective on the Sixties must acknowledge that a neatly coherent narrative of its history does not take into account one of the era's prime features — the nearly constant interaction between countercultural rebellion and political activism that blurred the distinction between the two. As they influenced and penetrated each other, these forces generated a dynamic, transformational energy that challenged just about every facet of American society, confronting militarism, nationalism, racism, sexism, consumerism, materialism, conformism. No less than *The New York Times* used the term "counterculture" in 1994 to encompass all of the movements of the 1960s in an editorial titled "In Praise of the Counterculture," saying that it

> profoundly altered the way Americans think about their inner lives, their fellow
> citizens, the earth upon which we live and the process by which older citizens in
> Washington decide when and where young Americans die in combat. . . . The spirit
> of the age, like the tactics of the antiwar movement, was shaped by the civil rights
> movement. Its lessons of citizen empowerment . . . led to the progress of the environ-
> mental, women's, and gay rights movements. The counterculture, in sum, produced
> a renewal . . . of the clear, defiant voice of the dissenting citizen.

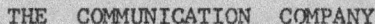

Haight/Ashbury

SURVIVAL SCHOOL

how to stay alive
on Haight Street

for
newcomers
& others

free!

classes & discussions
conducted by experts,
professional men &
experienced street kids

Every Monday night at 8

● The Scene
  where it's really at &
  what it is
● Drug Lore
  how to keep from getting
  killed for kicks
● Policemanship
  how to avoid getting busted
  & what to do if you are

Every Tuesday night at 8

● Sex Lore
  how to avoid gangbangs,
  rape, VD & pregnancy
● Health & Hygiene
  how to stay alive & well
● Street Wisdom
  how to avoid beatings &
  starvation, how to survive
  without money

a series of three classes
designed to save you from
becoming a psychedelic
casualty -- six months'
worth of knowledge in a
mere three days, & all free

free

no cheap moralizing,
no bullshit, nothing
phoney, no lies, no
beating around the bush,
no salestalk, just straight
information you can trust

Every Wednesday night at 8

● Haight Street Seminar
  experienced hippies & others
  rapping, answering questions,
  filling you in, telling it
  like it is, so you needn't be
  a helpless newcomer very long

-at-
THE TRIP WITHOUT A TICKET
901 Cole Street

San Francisco's Haight-Ashbury neighborhood (named for two intersecting streets) was a counter-cultural mecca for thousands of young people searching for an alternative lifestyle outside of the "9-to-5" world of "straight" jobs. "The Haight" was a lively area adjacent to Golden Gate Park, where emerging rock bands often gave free concerts. Marijuana and psychedelic drugs were readily available for experimenting with "consciousness expansion." The Haight's youthful adventurers, though, could be innocent and inexperienced, subject to manipulation and exploitation. The Survival School sought to prevent them from "becoming a psychedelic casualty."

The Panhandle, a part of Golden Gate Park near the Haight-Ashbury neighborhood, was the scene of many music events and other communal gatherings, planned and spontaneous. In 1967, a "Summer of Love" was anticipated, with thousands coming to the Haight. There was concern that this influx could escalate tensions between community residents and law enforcement authorities, and the Love Feast was likely an effort to reduce conflict by bringing residents and authorities together in a peaceful setting. (The term "heads" refers to those who regularly used psychedelic drugs such as LSD—lysergic acid diethylamide—or other mind-altering substances, including marijuana.)

A somewhat mysterious and vague announcement for a rock concert where you can "dance" and "freak," although no participating band or bands are specified, unless that is what the term "liquid" refers to. It appears that the admission price is a reasonable $1.00. The graphic portion could be interpreted as flowing water, thus possibly related to "liquid."

The Induction Center in Oakland, California, where men were processed for military service, was part of the horror of war perpetuated by America in Vietnam. In contrast to this evil, the 1968 Naked, Noisy Vigil for Peace and Love was a demonstration celebrating life in its purest form, represented by nudity. After all, "Naked people make love—people in uniforms make war." This leaflet is a clear example of how political activism and countercultural exuberance are combined in the same activity, with the naked figures embracing a peace symbol.

Sheep? Baa.

Beware of leaders, heroes, organizers: watch that stuff. Beware
of structure-freaks. They do not understand.
We know The System doesn't work because we're living in its ruins.
We know that leaders don't work out because they have all led us only
to the present, the good leaders equally with the bad. (Who caused
more suffering, Hitler or St. Paul?) It doesn't matter whether the
leader is good or bad: leading per se is bad. The medium is the
message, & the message of leadership is Vietnam. Concentration camps.
The Great Society. Riots on Haight Street.
What The System calls organization -- linear organization -- is a
Systematic cage, arbitrarily limiting the possible. It's never
worked before. It's always produced the present.
And heroes are only heroes, nothing more.
Any man who wants to lead you is The Man. Think: why would anyone
want to lead me? Think: why should I pay for his trip? Think.
LBJ is Our Leader, & you know where that's at.
Watch out for cats who want to play The System's games, 'cause
you can't beat The System at its own games, & you know that. Why
should we trade one Establishment for another Establishment?
Do your thing. Be what you are. If you don't know what you are,
find out.
Fuck leaders.

        A sound leader's aim
        Is to open people's hearts,
        Fill their stomachs,
        Calm their wills,
        Brace their bones
        And so to clarify their thoughts & cleanse their needs
        That no cunning meddler could touch them:
        Without being forced, without strain or constraint,
        Good government comes of itself.
                                        Lao Tzu

gestetnered 4/6/67 by the communication company (u.p.s.) be advised

This 1967 leaflet is not about an event, activity, issue, viewpoint, or agenda, but it is instead a statement of the cognitive freedom and liberation that happens with a complete rejection of conventionality ("The System") and the mental framework that justifies it: "The System doesn't work because we're living in its ruins. . . . What The System calls organization—linear organization—is a Systematic cage, arbitrarily limiting the possible." There is a joyful nihilism here, advocating a form of individual anarchism and self-determination totally detached from any prevailing social, cultural, or political norms and traditions: "Do your thing. Be what you are. . . . Fuck leaders."

SEX.... DRUGS ... GODS
IN THE TREE TRUNKS:
THE NEW
CONSCIOUSNESS
GUEST SPEAKER:
ED SANDERS,
Poet, Editor, Fug, Space Cadet
Lemar, League for Sexual
Freedom.
THURS. MAR. 10   12:15
GRAND BALLROOM (F101)
anarchist discussion group
CC.NY MAIN – DON'T LITTER

Ed Sanders, a founding member of the rock band The Fugs, was a bohemian rebel noted for his music, poetry, writing, progressive social activism, and exploration of altered forms of cognition. His decades of anti-establishment expression bridged the 1950s and 1960s, creatively merging politics with the counterculture. The title of his talk at the City College of New York in 1966 hints at an intersection of sensuality, psychedelics, and a primal environmentalism. Sanders is appearing at an Anarchist Discussion Group—is such a gathering possible? The leaflet features a basic drawing of what appears to be a visitor from another planet, perhaps the source of "The New Consciousness."

It's not really clear what was going to occur on Flower Power Day in Manhattan or exactly what would be done to "zap the military with love." There is a "peace and love" theme to the leaflet with flowers coming out of a tank. Political activism, combined with countercultural frivolity, will result in "DisArmed Forces Day." The tone is fanciful, whimsical, but also sobering: "Blow their minds, not their bodies," and "Don't let the generals and politicians make murderers of our brothers."

```
                  Position Paper of
    the Pacifist Anarchist Bisexual Psychedelic Conspiracy
                                                      α

To Those Who Want to Understand What We're Doing Here:

        Many people have come to us with questions like:
What do you stand for?  What are your demands?  You aren't
serious, are you?  How long will you stay?  Many are distraught
that we don't have pat answers and pat demands.  These ques-
tions show a well-trained (head fucked-over) academic mind.
You must classify, mustn't you?  Well here is your answer:
WE DON'T LIKE NROTC.

        For those of you who demand ideologies, structures,
demands, leaders:  well, we just won't cater to these hang-
ups.  There are many, many organizations on campus that will
provide you with pat answers:  also, just walk into any class-
room.  Most profs will be more than willing to preach rational
plastic to you again and again and again.

        We are a haven for those tired of the heavy scene
at Columbia.  For those of you who want further information
listen to the Beatles, smoke, read Revolution for the Hell of
It, drop, watch 8 1/2, smoke, dig the Incredible String Band,
groove, read Mr. Natural, fuck, listen to birds, eat, see Zorba
the Greek, smell, enjoy spring weather, touch, and sing some
songs with us.

the Pacifist Anarchist Bisexual Psychedelic Conspiracy.
```

Was the conspiracy an actual entity? Its name combines countercultural elements in a humorous, ironic manner. The leaflet's tone and content strongly suggest that this is a position paper without a position—other than heaping sarcasm on linear cognition, the habit of mental classification, the "academic mind," "rational plastic." ("Smoke" and "drop" refer to the use of marijuana and LSD, respectively. *Revolution for the Hell of It* was a book written by Abbie Hoffman, a notable political and cultural rebel during the Sixties. *8½* and *Zorba the Greek* are movies dealing with men having identity crises. Mr. Natural was an underground comic book character created by Robert Crumb.)

One of the central features of the counterculture was a rejection of organized Western religions for being overly formal, hierarchical, and dogmatic. There was instead a search for spiritual beliefs and practices that emphasized introspection, meditation, and connection with organic processes and nature. This search, though, was nonetheless conducted within an American context—"Krishna consciousness comes west"—and thus this 1967 mantra-rock dance features well-known rock bands alongside Swami Bhaktivedanta and Allen Ginsberg, a poet, deep ecologist, and cultural radical.

The leaders of the National Democratic Party are planning to meet in Chicago in August; there to enact, for the television audience, all the drama and excitement of an American Political Convention, culminating, it is understood, in the nomination of L. Johnson for President of the United States, and Leader of the Free World.

In the face of this act of sado-masochistic folly the free youth of America will simultaneously hold an enormous International Youth Festival in Chicago; there will be music playing and people swaying, dancing in the streets. Johnson and his delegates, locked in their slaughterhouse conventionhall theatre, will make ugly speeches and play ugly campaign music, while we, the living breathing youth of the world, will make the city a theatre, and every restaurant Alice's. Already, throughout parks and vacant lots in and around Chicago, agents of the Potheads' Benevolent Association have planted hundreds of thousands of pot seeds. The long hot summer of 1968 is expected to produce ideal weather for marijuana growing, and most of the crop should be ready for smoking by the end of August. F r e e people, free pot, free music, free theatre; a whole new culture will manifest itself to the world, rising from the ashes of America. Rock groups will be performing in the parks; newspapers will be printed in the streets; provos and police will play cops and robbers in the department stores; Democrats and dope fiends will chase each other through hotel corridors. Longboats filled with Vikings will land on the shores of Lake Michigan, and discover A m e r i c a ! Chicago will become a river of wild onions!

YOUTH INTERNATIONAL PARTY

CHICAGO, AUGUST 25-30, 1968

Yippee!

The Youth International Party ("Yippies") announced their intention to mark the occasion of the Democratic Party Convention, August 25–30, 1968, in Chicago, with an exuberant countercultural celebration and carnival featuring music, dancing, and free marijuana. The assumption that Lyndon Johnson will be nominated for a second term as President indicates that the leaflet was written before May 31 of that year, when he stunned the nation by saying he would not seek the nomination. The Yippies, reacting to the doctrinaire and sometimes self-important aspects of Sixties' radicalism, were intent on infusing politics with a heavy dose of humor, provocation, and rebelliousness.

RICHARD HERTZBERG attended the University of California, Berkeley, from 1963 to 1968, and lived in Berkeley until 1971. During this period Richard was an engaged member of Students for a Democratic Society, the Congress of Racial Equality, the Peace and Freedom Party, and Berkeley Ecology Action, and served as a community organizer in Oakland establishing tutorial programs for high-school students. From 1968 to 1978 he taught English, history, and social studies at alternative public high schools in California.

Motivated by a growing awareness of environmental issues, he then embarked on a forty-year career in the newly emerging profession of waste reduction, recycling, and materials conservation. He was one of the first consultants working in this field with both public entities and private companies.

Richard has written articles and opinion-editorials for such diverse publications as *BioCycle*, the *Los Angeles Herald-Examiner*, *Los Angeles Review of Books*, *Mother Earth News*, *New Age Journal*, *Resource Recycling*, and the *Oregonian*. He served as historical consultant to the Odyssey Theatre's widely acclaimed *The Chicago Conspiracy Trial* in Los Angeles (1979–1980), a dramatic production portraying the trial of several key organizers of demonstrations at the 1968 Democratic National Convention held in Chicago.

ROBERT COHEN is a professor of history and social studies at New York University. His books on the Sixties include *Freedom's Orator: Mario Savio and the Radical Legacy of the 1960s*; *Howard Zinn's Southern Diary: Sit-ins, Civil Rights, and Black Women's Student Activism*; and *Rebellion in Black and White: Southern Student Activism in the 1960s*.

JOHN LAURSEN earned degrees in political science from Reed College and UCLA in the late 1960s. In 1970 he founded Press-22, a Portland studio specializing in the editing and design of books and public-art typography. A 2020 recipient of the Oregon Governor's Arts Award, he is co-author of *Wild Beauty: Photographs of the Columbia River Gorge, 1867–1957*, and created the typographic design for the Oregon Holocaust Memorial.